Electronic Collaboration in Science

The Progress in Neuroinformatics Research Series
Series Editors: Stephen H. Koslow and Michael F. Huerta

Electronic Collaboration
in Science

Edited by

Stephen H. Koslow
Michael F. Huerta
National Institute of Mental Health

LEA **LAWRENCE ERLBAUM ASSOCIATES, PUBLISHERS**
2000 **Mahwah, New Jersey**   **London**

Lawrence Erlbaum Associates, Inc., Publishers
10 Industrial Avenue
Mahwah, New Jersey 07430

Cover design by Kathryn Houghtaling Lacey

Library of Congress Cataloging-in-Publication Data

Electronic collaboration in science/edited by Stephen H. Koslow and Michael F. Huerta.
    p. cm. — (Progress in neuroinformatice research; v.2)

Includes bibliographical references and index.
    ISBN 0-8058-3106-1 (hardcover : alk. paper)
    1. Communication in science—Technological innovations. 2. Research—Methodology. 3. Information technology. I. Koslow, Stephen H. II. Huerta, Michael F. III. Series.
    Q224.E44 2000
    507.2—dc2   99-053395

Printed in the United States of America
10 9 8 7 6 5 4 3 2 1

Contents

Foreword

Wm. A. Wulf
National Academy of Engineering

It is, perhaps, worth reminding ourselves that the laboratory—not the physical structure, but the social construct—is an invention, and that it is an invention that has profoundly changed the way that we do research in science and engineering. The laboratory evolved in early 19th-century Germany to support the principle of the unity of teaching, learning, and research—a principle to which we usually attach the name Wilhelm von Humboldt. By comingling a master with journeymen and apprentices in an inquiry-based teaching and learning environment, the researcher's methods, ethics, and passion for truth were conveyed along with the "mere facts." As it happens, the laboratory also enabled a scale of inquiry unattainable by the isolated, single researcher, and thus it changed the nature of the questions we dared to ask about nature, and the scope of artifacts we could attempt to build with that knowledge.

Some modern laboratories are huge by Humboldtian standards, as indeed is the whole research enterprise and its direct relevance to society. However, the laboratory has remained constrained and, in a sense, isolated by the demands of physical location. For quality communication, the participants need to be colocated. The instruments, the phenomena they measure, and the researchers who read the instruments needed to be similarly colocated. Access to the library of prior literature, the facilities for computation, and other analysis resources had to be close to the researchers.

The ubiquitous availability of high performance computers and telecommunications, collectively called *information technology*, has lessened these constraints of physical location. We are, perhaps, on the verge of the next great step in the evolution of the laboratory. And perhaps that step will have implications just as profound as the invention of the original construct—implications in terms of how we do research, what questions we even dare to ask, and what artifacts we have the courage to build.

From some future time, the long lens of history will tell us just how constraining and isolating the location was; we can't really know that now. But we can speculate that some multidisciplinary projects never happen because the "right people" don't happen to be colocated. We can speculate that an insight is never pursued because the person with the insight doesn't have access to the needed instrumentation. We can speculate that alternative hypotheses about a data set are not considered because, after reading a paper, the shear effort of obtaining the author's data is too large. We can speculate that the virtual demise of amateur research and the underutilization of fine minds in 4-year universities are related to their physical isolation from colleagues, instruments, and literature. We can speculate that the combined effect of the above is larger than the sum of them.

But before we speculate too much, and especially before we speculate about the possible impact of information technology, it is also worth reminding ourselves that despite all the changes it has already caused, those changes are probably pale precursors of the revolution that's still coming. Indeed, I expect that if these words are read 10 or 20 years into the 21st century, they will still be true. The speed of the improvement in the technology, combined with the slower social processes of change, virtually guarantees it.

To illustrate the kinds of change enabled by the technology, I routinely carry in my briefcase a computer 100 times more powerful than the Electronic Numberic Integrator and Calulator (ENIAC). Introduced in 1947, the ENIAC was the United States' first electronic digital computer. It used 18,000 vacuum tubes, weighed 30 tons, and filled a squash court-sized room. My briefcase demonstration is a greeting card that, when you open it, plays a tune. It contains a reasonably general-purpose microprocessor that has a clock speed 100 times that of the ENIAC. It cost $3 and was built to be thrown away. I can't guess what the demonstrator will be that I carry in 2020, but it is sure to be even better at making the point that speculation is almost sure to undershoot what we actually do with the technology.

However, I deeply believe that we can leverage the research enterprise enormously by using information technology to support collaborative virtual laboratories, or *collaboratories* as we have come to call them. It is only the precise shape of that leverage and the changes it will induce in the sociology of doing research, in the nature of the questions we ask, that seems unwise to speculate on. However, as with the greeting card, history suggests that we are more likely to undershoot than to overshoot the truth.

Modern research is incredibly instrument intensive, and sometimes my colleagues are inclined to view information technology as just another instrument. I think that is a fundamental mistake. In one way or another, those other instruments merely amplify our physical senses. They let us see further, or smaller, or in regions of the spectrum that our eyes do not respond to. They let us measure forces and masses that are too small, too large, or insufficiently different for our musculature to detect. And so on. In a way, these instruments are the logical extension of our 2 million years of history using tools that amplify our physical prowess. Information technology, however, is amplifying our intellectual prowess. That is very different. Just as happened with that other tool to amplify our intellect, writing, the future will be changed in unimaginably profound ways.

One last note—when we first coined the name *collaboratory*, I had in mind only the kinds of scientific and engineering research discussed in this volume. I have come to understand, however, that the concept is much more powerful and extends into scholarship of all kinds. Indeed, I now believe that humanistic scholarship is likely to be more profoundly affected by collaboratories than science and engineering in the early 21st century—but that is a story for another book.

Preface

Many fields of science operate in two, seemingly paradoxical, modes. The first, and fundamental, mode is highly individualistic. Scientific research requires exquisitely high levels of specialization, in terms of the area of knowledge and understanding possessed by the scientist as well as the tools used. For example, in the neuroscience community that includes some 50,000 scientists, it is not unheard of for only a handful of individuals to be considered experts in a particular aspect of a specific brain region in a given species. And, instrumentation, software, and other tools are commonly modified or even created de novo within a given laboratory to serve the highly specified purposes of the research conducted there. Thus, the first mode of operation for many areas of science is high specialization, and in many respects, insular.

In contrast, the second mode in which science operates is synthetic, bringing together the highly specialized knowledge of individual scientists and the singular capabilities of their tools and approaches to address the challenges posed by nature. Since nature is neither constrained by, nor concerned with disciplinary boundaries and other constructs that compartmentalize scientific knowledge, this synthetic mode of science is almost always required to create new knowledge and understanding. Nevertheless, successful synthesis of different areas of knowledge, different methodologies, etc., is neither trivial nor easy. A common vehicle to achieve this synthesis, of course, is collaboration across multiple laboratories. Not surprisingly, such collaborations are often with local colleagues, or with a very restricted pool of colleagues at distributed sites (restricted, in part, by the difficulty in maintaining collaborative interactions at a distance). These limited forms of collaboration have served science well. It is clear, however, that progress in science would accelerate if collaboration were not so constrained. It is tantalizing to imagine the scientific advances that could take place by removing or even relaxing limits to scientific collaborations, which, in turn, would result in increased synthesis across disciplines, perspectives, and approaches.

The Information Technology (IT) revolution, which has just begun, has already produced significant changes throughout society. In Biomedical Science, the Human Genome Project could not have been done with such relative ease were it not for bioinformatics. The time is propitious for other fields of science to harness these new technologies and the social changes they have engendered to facilitate scientific collaboration through electronic collaboratories.

The first publication in this series, *Neuroinformatics: An Overview of the Human Brain Project* (Koslow and Huerta, 1997) described the new emergence and incorporation of IT into the field of Neuroscience. This book explores several significant aspects of electronic collaboration in science. The Foreword, written by Wm. A. Wulf, who coined the term "collaboratory", provides an overview from the perspective of a pioneer and visionary in this area. The first chapter, written by Gary Olson and his colleagues, explores human behavior as it relates specifically to electronic collaboratories. An understanding of such behavior is key to whether the technological capabilities now available will actually be used by scientists, and how this use might be optimized. The second chapter, by Dan Burke, examines an increasingly important area for science: the issue of intellectual property rights. That chapter presents a discussion of how such rights might be appreciated and considered in electronic collaboratories. Peter Gray and Graham Kemp in the third chapter present technical aspects of data organization, storage and access. Case histories of particular, existing, electronic collaboratories in two different domains of the life sciences are presented by Graham Cameron and his colleagues and by Richard Kouzes in chapters 4 and 5, respectively. Finally, in chapter 6, Floyd Bloom and Warren Young examine the implications for electronic collaboration in the very diverse and rapidly advancing area of neuroscience.

It is our hope that this volume not only provides information to the reader, but also stimulates the growth of electronic collaboration in science. It allows for new ways for scientific collaboration, as well as novel approaches to deal with data in different ways. Our ability to manage information and data expeditiously will hasten our rate of knowledge growth leading to new discoveries and new solutions to problems. The affect of greatly increasing interactions across the many borders that separate scientists from novel data and perspectives would, no doubt, have unimaginable benefits for society at the dawn of the new millenium.

—*Michael F. Huerta*
—*Stephen H. Koslow*

REFERENCES

Koslow, S. H., & Huerta, M. F. (1997). *Neuroinformatics: An overview of the human brain project*. Mahwah, NJ: Lawrence Erlbaum Associates.

1 Behavioral Aspects of Collaboratories

Gary M. Olson
Thomas A. Finholt
Stephanie D. Teasley
University of Michigan

Collaboratories are a new form of human organization for the purpose of conducting team science (Finholt & Olson, 1997). Like laboratories, an organizational form that first flourished in the 19th century, they exist to further the advancement of science through providing scientists with access to other scientists, to information resources such as libraries and data bases, and to specialized instrumentation and their associated technical support. Both organizational forms—laboratories and collaboratories—are important training grounds for young scientists.

As science has become more collaborative, the organizational framework in which it takes place has become a critical determinant of progress. Major research centers and laboratories all over the world provide environments that have accelerated the pace of scientific advances. As the frontiers of knowledge are pushed back the problems get more and more difficult, often requiring large, complex teams—frequently multidisciplinary—to make progress. Exotic and expensive equipment or facilities can be justified only if they are designed and deployed collaboratively, maximizing their impact on a science community.

The collaboratory is emerging as a new option for the organization of scientific activity. The great contrast, of course, is that the key mediating principle of the laboratory is colocation, namely, having all of the human and material resources required for scientific research at a particular place. The collaboratory changes this by using communication and computing technology to relax the constraints of distance and time, and creating an instance of a virtual organization (Davidow & Malone, 1992; O'Hara-Devereaux & Johansen, 1994). Like all emerging virtual organizations, the collaboratory is both an opportunity with some very useful properties and also a challenge to human organizational practices. Many collaboratories have been attempted, but only a few have been successful as productive environments for advancing science.

There are two broad reasons for involving behavioral science in collaboratory projects, and we have considerable experience with both:

> • User-centered design. Effective information systems require sensitivity to users' needs and current practices (Norman & Draper, 1986; Olson & Olson, 1991, 1997), and the most effective means to assure good design is to interact with users during the design and deployment of new technologies. Ideally, design occurs iteratively, with recurring cycles of design, deployment, and empirical feedback (see Fig. 1.1). Failure to employ user-centered methods of system development is one of the most common reasons for the creation of ineffective collaboratories.
>
> • Longitudinal evaluation. Information technologies are built to serve human ends. Yet it often takes a long time for such technologies to be accepted and to have effects on the kinds of outcome measures that matter most to users. Long-term longitudinal studies of science practice are required in order to understand the effects of technologies on user behavior.

In this chapter we discuss each of these in more detail, drawing on our own experience with collaboratory design and deployment as well as drawing on the findings of others. We argue that both of these behavioral science purposes are critical to assure effective investments in collaboratories.

We will draw our discussion from a number of collaboratory projects, but since the most mature of those we have worked on is the Upper Atmospheric Research Collaboratory (UARC), we provide some background about the project.

THE UARC PROJECT: A BRIEF HISTORY

An important focus of space physics is the study of the earth's ionosphere, looking at the interactions of the terrestrial magnetosphere with the solar

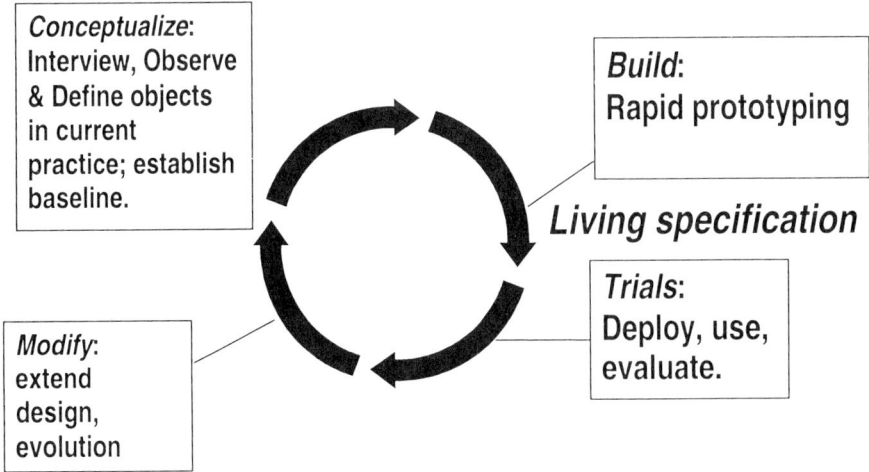

FIG. 1.1. User-centered iterative rapid prototyping strategy for design.

wind, and the resulting physical and chemical properties of the conducting atmosphere (Kelley, 1989). Space physics research depends heavily on observational data from ground-based facilities, from spacecraft, and from sounding rockets. In addition, the ambition of forecasting space conditions in the near earth environment, or *space weather*, has produced a need for increasingly comprehensive and accurate theoretical models—often computed with the use of super-computers.

The UARC project began by addressing the needs of scientists who used observational data collected from a suite of ground-based instruments at the Sondrestrom Upper Atmospheric Research Facility. The Sondrestrom facility is located on the west coast of Greenland above the Arctic Circle, and is jointly operated by the National Science Foundation and the Danish Meteorological Institute. UARC originally intended to provide remote access to real-time data from five Sondrestrom instruments, including the 60 meter incoherent scatter radar, an all-sky camera, a Fabry-Perot interferometer, an imaging riometer, and a local magnetometer. In addition, UARC aimed to support remote control of the all-sky camera and the Fabry-Perot interferometer. Safety concerns did not allow remote users to directly control the radar, but the remote principal investigators could initiate changes in the radar operation through interactions over the network with the site crew in Greenland. The imaging riometer and magnetometer operate continuously in unattended modes.

Between 1992 and 1995 UARC evolved to provide data viewers for all five of the instruments listed above. During this period, the primary use of the collaboratory involved real-time access to instruments at Sondrestrom, either for ionospheric observations or for instrument testing. At this early stage, collaboratory-based science resembled traditional research practices, although mediated by the Internet (see the detailed description of early UARC use in a later section). Early versions of UARC included limited collaboration support. For example, users could select their own parameters for data displays and then share these views via the collaboratory with other scientists (Prakash & Shim, 1994). In addition, a chat facility allowed users to enter text messages and broadcast them to other collaboratory users. And finally, UARC provided a data-oriented annotation capability that allowed users to describe or flag interesting phenomena for their colleagues. These features of the UARC system emerged through iterative design. That is, the UARC design strategy emphasized quick deployment of prototypes to the scientists, with resulting modifications based on feedback collected under conditions of actual use. The use of the NeXTStep programming environment, which provided excellent support for rapid user-interface development, strongly supported the iterative design approach.

Between 1995 and 1998 UARC transformed dramatically to accommodate three major changes that occurred during this period. First, early success with the collaboratory led to increased interest from scientists and demands to include more instruments. Unfortunately, the initial UARC architecture did not scale to accommodate increased numbers of users and instruments. Extensive testing revealed that UARC's centralized data distribution mechanism amplified delays caused by the Internet—and the impact of this effect increased as the number of users and instruments increased (Malan, Jahanian, & Knoop, 1997). The solution to this problem came in the form of a new UARC architecture that minimized data transmission bottlenecks through the use of multiple, distributed data servers (Hall, Mathur, Jahanian, Prakash, & Rassmussen, 1996). The new data transmission mechanism also provided a path for development of the Collaboratory Builders Environment, which provided a standardized basis for the development of applications that could be shared among many users (Lee, Prakash, Jaeger, & Wu, 1996).

Second, although the use of the NeXTStep environment initially accelerated UARC development, the requirement that scientists use an obscure operating system became a barrier to acceptance. Also, the rapid emergence and adoption of the World Wide Web suggested the importance of a web-based interface to UARC. To accommodate these needs, the core technology of UARC switched from NeXTStep to Java. In principle, the move to Java should have provided interoperability across a wide variety of computing platforms and better integration with emerging web resources. However, the transition proved exceptionally difficult. Browser and platform idiosyncrasies frustrated the promise of platform independence. Furthermore, instability of the

Java standard, such as the change from Java 1.0 to Java 1.1, forced major re-programming throughout the UARC system.

Third, having seen what might be possible with the early UARC system, the growing community of users began suggesting entirely new kinds of activities the collaboratory might support. In particular, three broad classes of new uses were suggested: (a) expansion of the data sources to produce a global "field-of-view" in real-time; (b) inclusion in real-time of theoretical model output side by side with observational data to (in the words of one UARC user) " ... close the data/theory loop;" and (c) use of the UARC technology to support distributed, retrospective workshops with the goal of producing publications based on collective analysis of interesting phenomena as viewed from multiple archival sources.

In 1998 UARC transformed into SPARC (Space Physics and Aeronomy Research Collaboratory). SPARC will continue with UARC's Internet and web strategy for providing collaboratory services, and will build on UARC's integration of real-time data, model predictions, and collaboration tools. SPARC will extend UARC's capabilities to archived data, collaborative workshops, and outreach to schools and the general public. In the following section we talk both about the experiences with UARC as well as with the planned extensions to SPARC.

OTHER COLLABORATORY PROJECTS

Although UARC/SPARC is our most sustained collaboratory project, and indeed, so far as we know, is the most long-term project (it will run for close to a decade, at least), it is not the only project we have done. For example, we have been involved in several recently launched projects in the biomedical area. We are working with the Pritzker Network, a research consortium spanning Michigan, Stanford, and the Cornell Medical Campus that focuses on a multidisciplinary approach to depression and mood disorders. We are a partner in the Great Lakes Center for Aids Research (CFAR) funded by NIH that links Minnesota, Wisconsin, Northwestern, and Michigan to pursue coordination clinical trials of emerging "cocktail" treatments for HIV infection. We were involved in several other unsuccessful attempts to launch collaboratory projects in the HIV arena that provided instructive lessons on the enabling conditions for collaboratory development. We were involved in a Medical Collaboratory project that introduced distributed tools for carrying out remote radiological consultations. Finally, we also participated in a series of collaboratory projects in industry, in which we have studied attempts to enable widely distributed teams within global corporations (Olson & Teasley, 1996). Although much of our discussion focuses on UARC, we draw some general lessons about collaboratory efforts from this broader experience base.

USER-CENTERED DESIGN

Many system developers agree that it is important to design information technology with users in mind. However, in actual practice, most technologies are designed with only the designers themselves consulted as potential users. Even when users are consulted, their needs and requirements are assessed superficially. One of the difficulties is that asking users what they need is a very poor way to design good software. Users are not particularly articulate about their work practices, in part because these practices are often embedded in individual and organizational routines that are tacit and difficult to see. The explication of such practices is often quite difficult. The result is technology that fails to meet the real needs of users, is very difficult to use, or has no long-term impact on indicators that are socially valued.

Many methods have been proposed to facilitate the development of effective and usable software (e.g., Nielsen, 1993; Olson & Moran, 1996; Shneiderman, 1997), and the evidence is encouraging that the use of such methods leads to better quality software. One method that has repeatedly yielded good results is iterative design with fairly tight cycles of design-development-deployment-evaluation (Landauer, 1995). We show this diagrammatically in Fig. 1.1.

We have used this strategy in our own collaboratory projects. A number of practical problems arise in carrying out such a strategy. Where does one start? How does one gather data for purposes of feedback? How does redesign proceed? What are the step sizes for successive generations of the software?

Our experience with UARC is instructive here. The goal of the UARC project was to enable Internet-based real-time data acquisition experiments in upper atmospheric physics. Early in the project we devoted much attention to the issue of how to extract user needs and how to refine the emerging system prototypes that were being deployed to real users (McDaniel, Olson, & Olson, 1994). We drew on concepts from human-computer interaction (e.g., Olson & Olson, 1997), object-oriented analysis and design (e.g., Jacobson, Christerson, Jonsson, & Overgaard, 1992), and business process reengineering (e.g., Hammer & Champy, 1993) to derive specific, concrete methods for moving from in-depth interactions with users to running code. We felt these methods enabled us to converge more quickly on useful and usable software, though the methods were not without their problems (see McDaniel et al., 1994, for details).

There is a major problem with this strategy that particularly plagues research-based deployments. The two biggest obstacles to user acceptance of software are the speed and reliability of the software itself. As systems become more complex or rely on emerging technologies for their implementation it becomes increasingly difficult to achieve levels of performance that are acceptable to users. If users will not use the software, it becomes difficult to ensure the empirical feedback required by the iterative software design process illustrated in Fig. 1.1.

The UARC project is a good example of these difficulties. The challenge of building reliable collaborative technology for the Internet during this period was enormous. The initial strategy adopted by the project in its earliest days of building within a proprietary environment (i.e., NeXTStep) ameliorated some of these problems. This environment also allowed for centralized system administration, which helped with version control and other technical coordination.

But as we migrated to a web-based strategy for the technology, these reliability problems increased. One technical challenge reflected the difficulty of providing continuous data flows from instruments that varied in reliability, data rate, and data volume. Network loads varied with time of day and geographic region, and sites varied in the quality of their connectivity to the Internet. These factors led to considerable work on the underlying data transport mechanisms and their interfaces with the Java applets that would display the data on the user's machine (Malan, Jahanian, & Subramanian, 1997). In the modified data transport system, users could select low, medium, or high "quality of service," or the policies to use for data delivery. For example, a user on a poor network connection could select low quality of service to ensure guaranteed arrival of a subset of available data with a preference for recent data (as opposed to selecting high quality of service, overwhelming the connection—and falling hopelessly out of synch with other scientists' viewers). In the future the quality of service provisions will be linked to automatic sensing of network load and client performance.

Another technical challenge resulted from the decision to use Java applets. In theory, Java should have provided platform independent code, accessible from any Java-enabled web browser (such as Netscape Navigator or Microsoft Internet Explorer). However, in practice the goal of platform independence remained elusive. A major problem involved the migration from the 1.0 version of the Java Development Kit (JDK) to the 1.1 version. Specifically, the dominant web browser vendors did not achieve compatibility with JDK 1.1 at the same rate or to the same degree. As a result, at times UARC could only run from those combinations of hardware and browsers guaranteed to be compatible with JDK 1.1. For instance, in October of 1997, UARC only worked with the HotJava browser on Solaris and Windows 95 platforms—whereas most scientists had Netscape Navigator installed on their computers. Although the situation improved by April 1998, even then UARC did not work with Microsoft Explorer on any platform or on Macintoshes with any browser. Even for those combinations that worked, users had to have updated versions of the browsers—sometimes with software patches installed—before they would work. This resulted in the need for considerable user support prior to and during the various major campaigns.

LONGITUDINAL EVALUATION

The impact of UARC on the practice of space physics was assessed longitudinally via active measures, such as regular administration of questionnaires about communication and collaboration, and unobtrusive measures, such as content analysis of chat, action, and network logs (e.g., McDaniel, Olson, & McGee, 1996). Several broad insights have emerged. When UARC started, scientists thought that the collaboratory would primarily support real-time space physics experiments. Expected benefits were framed in terms of reduced travel burdens, the ability to respond quickly to dynamic phenomena (e.g., solar flares), and increased access by students to data collection activity. All of these were achieved in the early years of UARC. As the UARC users became more familiar with the technology, however, a number of additional uses emerged, such as: (a) analysis of archived data in collaboratory-mediated workshops; (b) the simultaneous display of modeled and observed data; and (c) the integration of scores of previously independent instruments to produce real-time views of global scale phenomena. Our broad data collection effort in UARC allowed us to observe both expected and surprising results. Three specific areas were of interest to us.

Effects on Training and Education.   UARC offered a tantalizing view of how collaboratory use might change the course of graduate training in space physics. For example, use of UARC allowed students early participation as active members of research teams—in contrast to the traditional organization of space physics, where only the most senior students joined in data collection and analysis efforts. UARC extended the possibility of new kinds of research participation to a relatively small set of students. We see much potential to make this kind of participation possible for a significantly larger population with much greater diversity. A key focus of longitudinal data collection in SPARC, the successor to UARC, will be tracking of SPARC use and impact for graduate, undergraduate, and secondary students—both through unobtrusive measures (e.g., usage logs) and survey instruments.

Specifically, SPARC affords a kind of engagement with learning that has been described as "legitimate peripheral participation" (Lave & Wenger, 1991) or learning in a "community of learners" (Rogoff, 1994). Most of these theories, however, have arisen to describe activity in a shared physical setting. Less is known about how communities of learners might interact and instruct members via computer-mediated channels. Evidence from UARC suggests that students use contacts made via UARC to augment traditional access to mentors. The broader scope of SPARC will allow exploration of the usefulness of collaboratories in providing long-distance mentorship to budding scientists. Evidence of success may have important implications both for enticing more students to pursue science-related careers and in focusing practicing scientists on the importance of outreach activities for sustaining public interest in science.

Elaboration and Maintenance of Social Networks. Recent work in the sociology of science (e.g., Walsh & Bayema, 1996) points to the significance of the Internet as a mechanism in science for making and maintaining collegial ties. Yet, theorists have observed that the nature of these electronic ties differs from conventional ties (Wellman et al., 1996). Collaboratories represent virtual meeting places with great potential for generating serendipitous encounters that may escalate into substantial scientific collaborations. But, little is understood about how collaborations born and supported via computer networks fare relative to conventional collaborations. In the UARC experience, most collaborations predated the creation of the collaboratory. However, there were instances of interactions around data collection campaigns that suggested the potential for collaboratories as vehicles for bringing together scientist with complementary interests. For example, in February 1995, teams from the Lockheed Palo Alto Research Laboratory and from SRI International and the Florida Institute of Technology successfully interleaved unrelated experiments—and in the process, exposed members of each team to scientists they might otherwise have never encountered.

A key feature of collaboratory use is the rich array of use records generated by collaboratory participants, such as chat logs and server activity. The expanded scope of SPARC provides a broader basis for collecting behavioral data on scientific collaborations as they emerge and are sustained. These unobtrusive data will be augmented with more traditional social network questionnaires, such as name generators. Longitudinal data on the origin and fate of these computer-mediated collaborations will help inform our understanding of the potential of collaboratories to support substantive intellectual relationships—as measured in terms of research productivity and in terms of collaborators' satisfaction with computer-mediated interaction.

Emergence of New Organizational Forms. Science is a collaborative enterprise, and the traditional environment for scientific collaboration is the laboratory. Laboratories facilitate collaboration in two ways. First, as physical settings, laboratories provide scientists access to each other and to rare or expensive instruments (Allen, 1977; Hagstrom, 1965; Kraut, Egido, & Galegher, 1990; Pelz & Andrews, 1966). Second, as social organizations, laboratories certify and disseminate knowledge, train future generations of scientists, and produce agreement about scientific beliefs and practices (Knorr-Cetina, 1981; Latour, 1987; Latour & Woolgar, 1979; Lynch, 1985; Traweek, 1988). Recent developments in the evolution of information technology suggest that laboratories as physical settings may be less essential for scientific collaboration than were formerly the case, and that the collaboratory may be emerging as a new organizational form for science (Finholt & Olson, 1997). The indicators of this would include signs of institutionalization of collaboratory activities, including provisions for their continuity and long-term support, and changes in the social networks of practicing scientists (Walsh & Bayema, 1996; Wellman et al., 1996).

"READINESS" FOR COLLABORATORIES

Our broad experience with attempts at collaboratory projects has revealed that not all communities are ready for collaboratory technologies. There are two dimensions to this: collaboration readiness, and collaboration technology readiness.

Collaboration Readiness.   Readiness to collaborate or experience with collaboration is clearly the most basic prerequisite for an effective collaboratory. In UARC, we began the project with a community that had considerable experience with collaboration and major incentives to do so. Indeed, at some level, collaboration was built in to the social structure of the science. There was considerable specialization: Theory development versus data acquisition, and among those with a data focus, there was specialization by acquisition venue (ground-based, satellite) and even specific instrument type. The field had prespecified "rules of the road" for how data would be shared, and an infrastructure for creating data repositories. Coordinated Data Analysis Workshops (CDAWs) were operated by the National Space Science Data Center at Goddard Space Flight Center for the coordinated investigation of multiple satellite, multiple instrument investigations of particular geospace events. The CDAW workshops were held at NSSDC and a number of science teams met there to further investigate their data and coordinate the analysis and interpretation/understanding with other teams. This community was "collaboration ready."

In contrast, in some of the biomedical areas we have studied such collaboration readiness was not present at the outset. Much biomedical research is highly competitive, with both individuals and collocated laboratories working hard to be the first to achieve some breakthrough. In several cases, the lack of readiness was fatal to an effort to develop a collaboratory. In others, the collaborations themselves had to be brought along before technologies could be introduced with any expectation that they would take hold. Often the critical component to collaboration readiness was a real need that required working together in order to achieve a science goal. For instance, the need to enroll patients into clinical trials more quickly in order to make more rapid progress on the evaluation of treatment options was a major incentive in the Great Lakes CFAR. In the case of the Pritzker network of brain researchers, once they had agreed to work together they needed to devote special attention to the development of "rules of the road" for how data would be shared among the collaborators. In short, collaboration readiness has several broad components: motivation to collaborate, shared principles of collaboration, and experience with the specific elements of collaboration.

Collaboration Technology Readiness.   Collaboration technologies have been available as research prototypes for almost two decades, but it is only in the mid 1990s that a wide range of such technologies has begun to appear in products. For instance, e-mail was first used by researchers in the 1960s, but it has not become commonplace until the 1990s. More advanced collaborative technologies such as e-mail attachments, discussion databases, application sharing, and desktop video are still emerging in many communities.

Our experience with both science and industrial collaboratories is that there is a normal progression for the adoption of collaboratory technologies, shown in Fig. 1.2. Users unfamiliar with a simpler technology find it hard to grasp or adopt a more advanced one. Attempts to leapfrog this progression can often result in frustration or failure. Similarly, all collaborative technologies are deployed on a technology base that must be properly maintained and supported. Running effective networked infrastructure requires a nontrivial investment. These support issues increase as the technology becomes more sophisticated. For instance, in our experience the more advanced collaborative technologies in Fig. 1.2 require a considerable investment in training. Thus, early in a collaboratory project it is essential to assess the state of technology readiness in the community in order to ensure success. Again, several of our failed attempts to launch collaboratory projects were because the level of technology readiness in the relevant community was too primitive. The specific organizations neither had the experience or the base of technical support to advance very far in the progression of technologies shown in Fig. 1.2.

CONCLUSIONS

Collaboratories represent an exciting new opportunity for organizing scientific activity. There are encouraging signs from some of the long-standing collaboratory projects like UARC that the practice of science itself is on the threshold of transformation as a result of the adoption of the new technolo-

---

Technologies Requiring Minimal Training

  Electronic Mail

  Electronic Mail with Formatted Attachments

  Using Repositories

  Group Calendaring

Technologies Requiring Training in Both Collaboration and the Tools

  Creating Repositories

  Hand-off Collaboration

  Synchronous collaboration

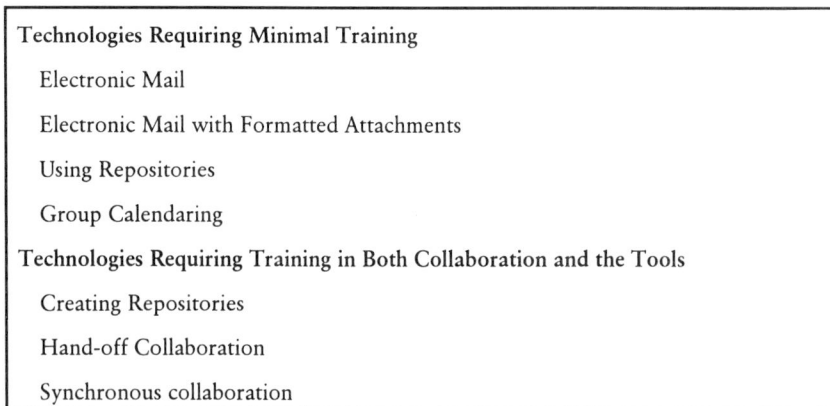

FIG. 1.2. Hierarchy of collaborative technologies.

gies. However, there are many obstacles to the successful design of collaboratories that have a measurable effect on the productivity of a science. An accurate assessment of the readiness of a community for both collaboration and technologies and the adoption of iterative, user-centered design methods can help. As sophisticated collaboration tools migrate from the laboratory into products, the level of readiness among scientists can only increase. Furthermore, the complexity of scientific problems and the increasing need for specialized instrumentation and resources will encourage a climate of collaboration. We expect the collaboratory will become as common as the laboratory, and that longitudinal studies of their effectiveness will reveal significant impacts of such organizations on the practice of science.

ACKNOWLEDGMENTS

The research reported in this chapter was supported by NSF cooperative agreement IRI-9216848, NSF grant ATM-9873025, NIH grant 1P30 CA 79458-01, and grants from the John D. Evans Foundation, the Nancy Pritzker Depression Research Network, IBM, Ford Motor Co., Lucent Technologies, and Bell Labs Research.

REFERENCES

Allen, T. J. (1977). *Managing the flow of technology*. Cambridge, MA: MIT Press.

Davidow, W. H., & Malone, M. S. (1992). *The virtual corporation: Structuring and revitalizing the corporation for the 21st century*. New York: Harper Collins.

Finholt, T. A., & Olson, G. M. (1997). From laboratories to collaboratories: A new organizational form for scientific collaboration. *Psychological Science, 8,* 28–36.

Hagstrom, W.O. (1965). *Scientific community.* New York: Basic Books.

Hall, R.W., Mathur, A., Jahanian, F., Prakash, A., & Rassmussen, C. (1996). Corona: A communication service for scalable, reliable group collaboration systems. *Proceedings of the ACM 1996 Conference on Computer-supported Cooperative Work* (pp. 140–149). New York: ACM Press.

Hammer, M., & Champy, J. (1993). *Reengineering the corporation: A manifesto for business revolution.* New York: Harper Collins.

Jacobson, I., Christerson, M., Jonsson, P., & Overgaard, G. (1992). *Object-oriented software engineering: A use case driven approach.* Reading, MA: Addison-Wesley.

Kelley, M. C. (1989). *The Earth's Ionosphere: Plasma Physics and Electrodynamics.* New York: Academic Press.

Knorr-Cetina, K. (1981). *The manufacture of knowledge: An essay on the constructivist and contextual nature of science.* New York: Pergamon.

Kraut, R., Egido, C., & Galegher, J. (1990). Patterns of contact and communication in scientific research collaboration. In R. Kraut, C. Egido, & J. Galegher (Eds.), *Intellectual teamwork: Social and technological foundations of cooperative work* (pp. 149–171). Hillsdale, NJ: Lawrence Erlbaum Associates.

Landauer, T. K. (1995). *The trouble with computers: Usefulness, usability, and productivity.* Cambridge, MA: MIT Press.

Latour, B. (1987). *Science in action.* Cambridge, MA: Harvard University Press.

Latour, B., & Woolgar, S. (1979). *Laboratory life: The social construction of scientific facts.* London: Sage.

Lave, J., & Wenger, E. (1991). *Situated learning: Legitimate peripheral participation.* Cambridge, UK: Cambridge University Press.

Lee, J. H., Prakash, A., Jaeger, T., & Wu, G. (1996). Supporting multi-user, multi-applet workspaces in CBE. *Proceedings of the ACM 1996 Conference on Computer-supported Cooperative Work* (pp. 344–353). New York: ACM Press.

Lynch, M. (1985). *Art and artifact in laboratory science.* London: Routledge & Kegan Paul.

Malan, G. R., Jahanian, F., & Knoop, P. (1997). Comparison of two middleware data dissemination services in a wide-area distributed system. *Proceedings of the 17th IEEE International Conference on Distributed Computing Systems* (pp. 411–419). Los Alamitos, CA: IEEE Computer Society Press.

Malan, G. R., Jahanian, F., & Subramanian, S. (1997). Salamander: A push-based distribution substrate for Internet applications. *Proceedings of the USENIX Symposium on Internet Technologies and Systems* (pp. 171–181). Berkeley, CA: The USENIX Association.

McDaniel, S. E., Olson, G. M., & McGee, J. C. (1996). Identifying and analyzing multiple threads in computer-mediated and face-to-face conversations. *Proceedings of CSCW '96'* (pp. 39–42). New York: ACM Press.

McDaniel, S. E., Olson, G. M., & Olson, J. S. (1994). Methods in search of methodology—Combining HCI and object orientation. *Proceedings of CHI '94* (pp. 145–151). ACM Press.

Nielsen, J. (1993). *Usability engineering.* New York: Academic Press.

Norman, D. A., & Draper, S. W. (Eds.). (1986). *User centered system design*. Hillsdale, NJ: Lawrence Erlbaum Associates.

O'Hara-Devereaux, M., & Johansen, R. (1994). *Global work: Bridging distance, culture & time*. San Francisco: Jossey-Bass.

Olson, J. S., & Moran, T. (1996). Mapping the method muddle: Guidance in using methods for user interface design. In M. Rudisill, C. Lewis, P. B. Polson, & T. McKay (Eds.), *Human-computer interface design: Success Cases, emerging methods, and real world contexts* (pp. 269–302). New York: Morgan Kaufman.

Olson, G. M., & Olson, J. R. (1991). User-centered design of collaboration technology. *Journal of Organizational Computing, 1*, 61–83.

Olson, G. M., & Olson, J. S. (1997). Research on computer-supported cooperative work. In M. G. Helander, T. K. Landauer & P. V. Prabhu (Eds.), *Handbook of human-computer interaction* (2nd ed., pp. 1433–1456). New York: Elsevier.

Olson, J. S., & Teasley, S. (1996). Groupware in the wild: Lessons learned from a year of virtual collocation. *Proceedings of the ACM 1996 Conference on Computer-supported Cooperative Work* (pp. 419–427). New York: ACM Press.

Pelz, D. C., & Andrews, F. M. (1966). *Scientists in organizations: Productive climates for research and development*. New York: Wiley.

Prakash, A., & Shim, H. S. (1994). DistView: Support for building efficient collaborative applications using replicated objects. *Proceedings of the ACM 1994 Conference on Computer Supported Cooperative Work* (pp. 153–164). New York: ACM Press.

Rogoff, B. (1994). Developing understanding of the idea of communities of learners. *Mind, Culture, and Activity, 1*, 209–229.

Shneiderman, B. (1997). *Designing the user interface: Strategies for effective human-computer interaction* (3rd ed.). Reading, MA: Addison-Wesley.

Traweek, S. (1988). *Beamtimes and lifetimes: The world of high energy physics*. Cambridge, MA: Harvard University Press.

Walsh, J. P., & Bayema, T. (1996). Computer networks and scientific work. *Social Studies of Science, 26*, 661–703.

Wellman, B., Salaff, J., Dimitrova, D., Garton, L., Gulia, M., & Haythornthwaite, C. (1996). Computer networks as social networks: Collaborative work, telework, and virtual community. *Annual Review of Sociology, 22*, 213–238.

2 Intellectual Property Issues in Electronic Collaborations

Dan L. Burk
University of Minnesota

Intellectual property law increasingly has become part of the backdrop for scientific research. Both the fruits of research and the tools used to obtain those fruits may be the subject of patent, copyright, trade secrecy, or other proprietary rights. Anticipating the impact of such laws, and sorting out the competing proprietary interests may prove to be a challenge for scientific collaboration, and especially for "virtual" collaborations that take advantage of emerging digital technologies. Consequently, this chapter surveys the law of intellectual property as it applies to such technologies, with particular emphasis on the types of intellectual property issues likely to arise in collaborative scientific research.

We must recognize from the outset that an undertaking in the nature of this chapter topic may seem impossibly ambitious. First, no comprehensive review of the topic, which could itself be the subject of an extensive book, or perhaps a treatise of several volumes, is possible in relatively few pages. Second, the topic stands at the intersection of two highly dynamic fields of endeavor; given the rapidity of change for both the relevant law and technology, there is a substantial danger that the details of any review may become dated in a relatively short time. Finally, intellectual property law by itself is an extremely specialized area that encompasses the almost metaphysical subtleties of owning intangibles. This body of law challenges the seasoned practitioner, let alone those readers who may be uninitiated into its mysteries.

However, it is possible in this space to describe basic concepts, to alert collaborative researchers to potential issues, and to identify certain important trends that will effect the conduct of research. Accordingly, the first part of this chapter reviews the basic forms of intellectual property law relevant to collaborative research in a digital environment, suggesting the likely applications of such law. The chapter then turns to certain themes underlying this smorgasbord of different laws, giving particular attention to the differing value systems of scientific research and of intellectual property law, and highlighting the tensions inherent in the incentives of collaborative electronic research. Finally, the chapter uses the underlying structure of values and incentives to discuss a series of emerging legal issues that are likely to impact research conducted in networked environment.

One or two caveats are necessary to define the scope of the discussion. This chapter focuses primarily on U.S. law, with appropriate references to comparative issues in other parts of the world. I have adopted this approach in large part because of the impossibility of reviewing the law of every nation that might effect electronic collaborators; the transborder nature of digital networks guarantees that the law of every nation could be relevant. Of the many sets of national law that might be relevant, U.S. law is an appropriate choice for focus because of the significant lead that the United States currently enjoys in the development of legal precedent related to digital networks. A critical mass of digital network users within the United States has generated a robust body of early precedent, and these decisions have tended to shape the resolution of similar issues in the rest of the world. Other nations that have begun to grapple with issues already decided in the United States have turned to U.S. precedent for guidance in their own decisions. Thus, we may expect that "cyberlaw" around the world will for some time reflect decisions now being made in U.S. law.

But despite the choice of focus on a representative body of law, the international dimension of the issues discussed here is profound and pervasive. The trend toward globalization is far too significant to be ignored, and probably cannot be overemphasized. This is not merely because other nations are beginning to amass their own unique bodies of legal precedent that will compete with U.S. law in shaping the development of global computer networks. Rather, the juxtaposition of differing legal regimes via electronic collaboration holds the potential for conflict. The substantive laws regarding copyrights, patents, and other proprietary rights may vary significantly from nation to nation, and these differences may potentially generate conflicts among electronic collaborators. As an example, the unwitting activity of one collaborator from a particular jurisdiction in disclosing research results may preclude the opportunity to obtain a patent on those results in other jurisdictions. (Burk, 1994b). Such potential conflicts have long been part of international collaborations, but the increased opportunity for collaborations afforded by digital media will tend to increase their incidence.

However, electronic collaboration may do more than simply exacerbate the problems of past collaborative activity. Online collaborations may pose difficult and unique questions regarding legal jurisdiction and choice of law. (Ginsburg, 1995). When activities have a definite physical situs, it is usually obvious which jurisdiction's law might govern the activity. But where researchers from different nations are engaged in electronic collaboration, it may be difficult or impossible in advance to determine which nation's intellectual property law should govern their efforts. (Geller, 1996). Thus, research results developed in a virtual "collaboratory" could be subjected to the law of many different nations. Similarly, participants in international "collaboratory" efforts may have difficulty determining whether the research tools they use infringe the rights of third parties in any of the nations that might assert legal authority over the effort. (Burk, 1993). Scientists in electronic collaborations should be aware of such issues, but they cannot be resolved in the few pages available here.

In addition to the national constraints of the discussion, this chapter focuses primarily on modes of intellectual property protection that are explicitly designated as such: patents, copyrights, trade secrets, and related topics. But these legal categories comprise only a small subset of the law that is likely to effect electronic collaboration; many other important issues are necessarily excluded from this review. For example, laws now being implemented in the European Union countries impose a high degree of privacy protection on individualized data collected in those countries, and forbid the transborder flow of such data to countries with lesser levels of protection. Under certain circumstances, researchers in an international electronic collaboration could well be affected by such prohibitions. These privacy laws could be considered a type of proprietary interest granted to individuals in data concerning themselves, but are not considered here. Rather, we begin with an overview of the major existing categories of intellectual property law.

Patents

Patents are exclusive rights granted by the federal government to the inventors of new and useful machines, articles, substances, or processes. The patent right is offered in return for full disclosure by inventors as to how to make and use their patented invention. Unlike other forms of intellectual property such as copyrights and trademark rights, patent rights do not arise spontaneously. Patents only issue after an administrative application procedure in the U.S. Patent Office. The inventor must submit an application that fully describes and explains the invention, and which sets out the limits of technology being claimed. This description will form the basis for the published patent once the application is approved. If the patent is granted, a full description of the invention and its use is published by the government in the patent. These published patent disclosures form a fund of knowledge for the public. The term of the exclusive right lasts for 20 years from the date that the application is filed, and at the end of the patent term, the invention passes into the public domain, that is, anyone may freely use it.

As in the case of most intellectual property, including copyright and trademarks, there is no such thing as a worldwide patent. Successful applications to the U.S. Patent Office will result in a patent that is good only in the United States. If the inventor desires patent protection in other countries, he or she must apply for a patent in the patent office of each country where a patent is wanted. The expense of so many patent applications may be prohibitive, so inventors must frequently be selective as to the countries in which they wish to apply. The countries in which an inventor chooses to apply will be determined by his or her long range business plan; usually, the inventor will choose to apply for patents in the countries where he or she is most likely to license the invention.

Inventors who desire a patent must be extremely careful about their activities prior to applying for the patent. The United States gives an inventor a 1-year grace period to apply for a patent after an invention has been publicly disclosed. The clock on this grace period will start running if an inventor places the invention on sale, publishes a description of the invention, offers a detailed description of the invention at a public meeting, or otherwise places the invention into the hands of the public. If the inventor does not apply for a patent within a year of such a public disclosure, then the opportunity to obtain a patent is permanently lost—there is no reason to offer an incentive to share the invention with the public if the inventor has already done so.

However, the United States is unusual in offering the inventor a 1-year grace period after public disclosure of the invention. Almost all other countries in the world give no grace period: Once the invention is publicly disclosed, the chance to obtain a patent is irretrievable lost. Consequently, an accidental or even deliberate public disclosure of the invention could leave an inventor with only the opportunity for a U.S. patent. Significantly, the growth of digital media, by increasing the opportunity for communication between researchers, has heightened the likelihood of inadvertent disclosure of otherwise patentable inventions.

The United States is also unusual in granting patents to the first person to invent the invention. Sometimes two inventors will develop identical inventions at about the same time. The majority of countries will grant the patent for such an invention to the inventor who files his or her application first. The United States will usually grant the patent to the inventor who applies first unless a subsequent inventor can prove that he or she invented the invention before the first applicant. U.S. Patent Office proceedings to determine priority of invention are called interferences. They are complicated legal contests, similar to litigation, and may take years to resolve.

Additionally, U.S. law requires that a patent bear the name of the inventor of the claimed invention, even if the inventor was working for another at the time of the invention. Employees of a corporation or university are frequently required to assign their patents to their employer as a condition of employment. Sometimes the employer may agree to share royalties with the employee, or offer a bonus or other reward in exchange for the assignment of the rights in the patent. However, no matter what type of arrangement the inventor may have with the employer, the employer's name cannot be substituted for that of the inventor on the patent.

In the context of collaborative electronic research, patent rights may be implicated at different levels of research and of discovery. The exclusive rights granted with a patent include the right to exclude others from "use" of the claimed invention, including most uses in research. Thus, in some instances, questions of patent infringement may arise with regard to the use of patented software, hardware, or processes as research tools. At a different level, patent issues may arise regarding the inventorship and ownership of tangible results generated from the collaboration. Collaborators can potentially interfere with one another's patent rights, for example by prematurely publicly disclosing the invention in a scientific conference. This may be a particular problem in electronic collaboration, given the ease of online disclosure via e-mail or electronic conferencing, and especially in international collaborations where the applicable law may differ between collaborators. Thus, a clear understanding of the goals and ground-rules for any collaborative research are essential before the collaboration is undertaken.

Copyrights

Copyright covers literary works such as books, plays, and poems; musical works; sound recordings; pictorial and graphic works such as paintings, drawings, cartoons and photographs; and audiovisual works, such as motion pictures and graphic animation. Additionally, copyright covers computer software, which is considered a kind of literary work. Copyright also covers the original selection and arrangement of collections or compilations. Thus, a great deal of the content found in digitized formats falls within the subject matter of copyright.

Copyright does not cover facts, short phrases or words, ideas, processes, or unfixed works. For example, an improvisational theater performance or musical "jam session" will not be covered by copyright if it is not recorded, because it is an unfixed work. Similarly, a measurement or a law of nature cannot be copyrighted because they are facts that did not originate from an author, but that simply exist as part of the world. Business names or book titles usually are not copyrightable because they are short phrases or words. Recipes and game rules usually are not copyrightable because they simply describe processes.

The fundamental premise of copyright law is the distinction between a copy and the work. The work is the abstract, intangible, intellectual good that is embodied in a tangible copy. Copyright confers on the copyright holder the right to control reproduction, distribution, adaptation, public performance, and public display of the work, but does not necessarily grant the copyright holder rights in a particular copy. This dichotomy is perhaps best illustrated in copyright's "First Sale" doctrine. The purchaser of a particular copy does not by virtue of the purchase gain rights in the work. The copyright in the work still rests with the author or copyright owner, so the purchaser of the copy is still precluded from, for example, reproducing the work by creating additional copies embodying the work. But the purchaser does generally have the right to dispose of his copy as he wishes, by reselling it, giving it away, or even destroying it. The copyright owner may, of course, also sell the copyright to the work, but that is a different matter from selling copies of the work.

Unlike patents, copyrights arise spontaneously when the work is fixed. As soon as pen is set to paper, or brush to canvas, or fingers to keyboard, the resulting work is automatically copyrighted. No application or registration is necessary. The work may be registered with the Copyright Office if the author wishes, but this is optional. There are benefits for choosing to register the work, in particular, the copyright cannot be enforced in a U.S. court unless it has been registered. In the United States, copyright lasts for different periods of time, depending on who the author may be. The copyright term for a work created by a natural person is the lifetime of the author plus 70 years. The copyright term for a work created by a corporation, through its employees, is 120 years from the date of creation, or 95 years from the date of publication. After a copyright expires, the work falls into the public domain for anyone to use.

Copyright may also vest in more than one author, depending on the circumstances under which a work is created, and such authorship rules may be particularly important in collaborative research. If two or more individuals create an integrated copyrightable work, they are considered joint authors, with equal rights to the entire work. Alternatively, if someone alters or adapts a previously existing work, a derivative work is created in which each author may have rights to his or her original contribution to the final product—it is worth noting that if the adaptation of the work is unauthorized, the act of creating the derivative work can be an infringement of the first author's copyright. Finally, in the case of a compilation such as an anthology, each contribution may be the subject of an individual copyright, whereas the original selection and arrangement of the collection may be the subject of a copyright to the anthology as a whole.

As in the case of patents, there is no international copyright or universally recognized copyright; copyright exists nation by nation. However, unlike the case of patents, many nations are signatories to an international treaty, the Berne Convention, which sets minimum standards for copyright protection, and requires nations to accord the citizens of other signatory nations the same rights that it gives to its own citizens. Additionally, the standards of the Berne convention have been adopted as part of the series of intellectual property treaties accompanying membership in World Trade Organization. Consequently, the basics of copyright are similar among most nations, although variations are possible.

The copyright law provides for an important limited right called "fair use" that allows unauthorized use of portions of the copyrighted work for certain select purposes. The fair use privilege is especially important in allowing study, scholarship, commentary, and criticism of copyrighted works. For example, quoting a few lines of a book in a book review would be a classic example of fair use. Without the fair use privilege, copying the lines out of the book would constitute infringement, and could not be done without the permission of the copyright owner.

Trademarks

Trademarks are names, logos, designs, emblems, or other identifying marks that distinguish goods or services. Even distinctive sounds and smells can be trademarks. To be a trademark, the mark must be identified in the minds of consumers with a particular source of a good or service. Closely to related trademark law is the law of trade dress protection. Trade dress encompasses the identifiable packaging or presentation of products and is protected under law resembling that for protection of trademarks. Trade dress protection may even extend to the distinctive decor of a restaurant. In the United States, trademarks and trade dress are protected under both state and federal law.

A primary goal of both trademark and trade dress law is to protect consumers. If competing businesses use identical or similar marks, consumers may be confused as to which business they are dealing with or purchasing from. Consumer confusion could be a particular problem if a consumer believes he or she has purchased goods of a certain quality, but mistakenly receives goods of a lesser quality. The distinguishing features of the trademark or trade dress assist consumers in accurately identifying the quality of goods they wish to pay for.

Trademark law also helps to deter business fraud in which a dishonest business intentionally tries to pass off its goods as those of another. This not only protects consumers, but also protects the customer goodwill and reputation of businesses. Businesses may invest a great deal of time and money in developing high quality products and favorable customer relations. However, if lower quality goods are passed off as those of a known business, consumers may be angry or dissatisfied and blame the business they thought they were dealing with, damaging that business' reputation.

Trademarks are not as often implicated in basic scientific research as patents and copyrights because the fruits of scientific research are not directly aimed at consumers. However, researchers themselves are consumers of research related products and services. As a consequence, trademark disputes do occasionally arise in the context of scientific discourse, as for example in a commercial chemical manufacturer's assertion of trademark rights in the use of term *taxol* rather than *paclitaxel* to refer to a microtubule disaggregating agent derived from the Pacific Yew tree. In the digital environment, similar disputes have arisen over common use of the term *listserv* to refer to Internet mail exploder software, and over the use of Internet domain names that incorporate well known product or service names. Given that trade dress protects the look and feel of products including the interior of retail stores, one might also expect future trade dress disputes over interfaces for collaborative research software, particularly those with a distinctive three dimensional or virtual reality aspect.

Trade Secrets

Trade secrets can be any type of information, process, idea, or "know how" that is not generally known and that gives the possessor an advantage in the marketplace. Trade secrets therefor include a wide range of confidential business information. Chemical formulas, industrial processes, business plans, and customer lists are common examples of trade secrets. Trade secret law is primarily state law, and may vary slightly from state to state. Additionally, Congress has recently passed a federal criminal statute that is designed protects the trade secrets of U.S. companies from industrial espionage.

In order to maintain business information as a trade secret, a business must take reasonable precautions to prevent the information from becoming generally known to its competitors. Such reasonable precautions could include revealing business information to employees only on a "need to know" basis, keeping sensitive documents under lock and key, requiring passwords to access computer files, restricting access to certain areas of production facilities, requiring that visitors to the facilities sign in on arrival and sign out on departure. Employee education is also a key part of trade secret management. Employees in commercial firms are trained to take care with proprietary information, and warned about what business information is proprietary and what information is not.

The law of trade secrecy deters industrial espionage by penalizing the efforts of competing businesses to learn one another's proprietary information by improper means. Improper means of acquiring a trade secret might include infiltrating a competitor's production facility, stealing a competitor's documents, or bribing a competitor's employees. However, trade secrecy law does not prohibit a competitor from reverse engineering a product sold on the open market, or from independently developing the secret. Reverse engineering and independent development are considered legitimate means of acquiring a competitor's business information. Consequently, products that are mass-marketed, or that otherwise lend themselves to reverse engineering are poor candidates for trade secret protection. Trade secrecy is more typically employed to protect industrial processes or other knowledge that can be withheld from public distribution.

In a business setting, trade secrecy can also be a particular concern when employees change jobs, or leave a company to start their own business. The employee will likely know many trade secrets of the previous employer, and may consciously or unconsciously use that information in his or her new job. Cautious employers will conduct entrance and exit interviews with employees, in order to control and minimize trade secret transfer. Entrance interviews can be used to inform and educate employees about trade secrets they may encounter in their new position; the entrance interview can also be used to limit the new employer's liability by warning new employees not to use proprietary knowledge gained from previous employment at the new job. Exit interviews can be used to review what the employer considers proprietary, and to admonish the departing employee not to use such knowledge in their new job. Some employers will also make confidentiality of trade secrets an express condition of their employees' employment contract; such contractual terms can be reviewed in the entrance and exit interviews.

Of all the intellectual property regimes discussed here, trade secrecy may be the least compatible with expectations of scientific collaboration, because it contemplates restrictions on the sharing of information with the public, and even with fellow collaborators. This is also the form of intellectual property most difficult to maintain in an electronic research environment. Trade secrecy is likely to be compromised by the easy reproducibility and transferability of digitized information. Conversely, efforts at maintaining reasonable secrecy, such as password protection, data encryption, or requiring collaborators to sign confidentiality agreements, would likely hamper full collaboration in an electronic environment.

The Public Goods Problem

The proprietary regime of trade secrecy well illustrates the problems of restriction on the free flow of information most characteristic of trade secrecy, but which are to some extent endemic to all forms of intellectual property protection. The explanation for these restrictions in the generally accepted rationale for intellectual property arises out of the peculiar economics of information, which resemble economic *public goods*. Public goods are defined as those goods that display the qualities of nonexclusivity and nonrivalrous consumption. A classic textbook example of such a public good is national defense: Once a unit of national defense has been generated, its benefits can be simultaneously enjoyed by many people, and indeed it is difficult to prevent people within a certain geographic or political region from enjoying those benefits. These attributes are radically different from those displayed by a private good, such as a banana, which cannot be consumed by more than one individual at once, and from which people can be excluded by hiding it, guarding it, or fencing it.

From an economic standpoint, the unusual attributes of public goods may lead to so called *market failures*, or problems in their private production and distribution. The exclusive nature of private goods ensures that consumers can be made to pay for them; if there is no payment, the goods may be withheld. Fencing of tangible property such as an amusement park or parking garage allows the owner to condition access to the property on payment of a fee. However such fees are difficult to levy for intangible goods because fencing them off is difficult; because they are nonexclusive, people can enjoy them without paying for them—once the goods exist, they cannot be withheld. Thus, it may be difficult to induce people to pay for something like national defense, because they will be inclined to hope that they can enjoy it for free once someone else pays for it. This in turn suggests that national defense may be undersupplied; no one will be willing to undertake the cost of producing it, knowing in advance that no one will pay for it once it comes into existence. In the particular case of national defense, we therefor have developed a system of compelled payment—called taxes—in order to ensure payment.

In their purest form, information goods display qualities similar to those of a classic public good. A song, story, or idea can be reproduced and disseminated at a marginal cost approaching zero by the simple expedient of singing or relating the information to other people. Because of their intangible nature, such pure information goods do not even incur the transportation costs that would be required to disseminate physical goods. As a consequence, just as in the case of national defense, we might expect valuable information to be undersupplied: Because the information can be cheaply reproduced and distributed, it is essentially nonexclusive. A potential creator will realize beforehand that it will be difficult or impossible to induce people to pay for the song or idea. With no possibility to recoup the investment, we might expect creative thinkers and artists to be reluctant to make the investment necessary to develop valuable information.

Intellectual property laws attempt to solve this problem of disincentive by creating exclusive rights in valuable information—essentially, creating legal fences around creative works, allowing a creator to legally exclude potential consumers, even if physical exclusion from the creative work is impossible. The law therefore attempts to provide creators of intangible goods with a legal fence in the form of a patent or copyright. The fence takes the form of a period of exclusivity, during which no one is permitted to replicate the work without the creator's permission. The creator may premise permission on a fee, if he wishes, allowing him to recover the costs of creating the work. If consumers do not obtain permission to use the fenced information, legal coercion in the form of an infringement lawsuit will be applied to force them to pay. Because creators know that such legal fencing will allow them recover their investment costs, they will be more likely to make the initial investment, leading to more production of creative intangible goods.

Careful consideration of the solution to the public goods problem reveals an inherent contradiction in this system of incentives: The system seeks to make available more intellectual goods, but this is accomplished by fencing off goods that people could otherwise freely enjoy. Like any other kind of fence, copyrights, patents, and other intellectual property are clearly restrictions on the availability of informational goods, and will allow intellectual property owners to raise the price of access beyond the price that some consumers can pay. Stated differently, the ethos of intellectual property restricts the availability of informational goods in order to ensure that there are informational goods in the first instance. This implies that the intellectual property right cannot be justified when the disutility of restriction exceeds the utility of the information generated under the system. Thus, intellectual property law continually walks a social policy tightrope, attempting to balance the degree of incentive offered against the degree of restriction imposed.

It should also be apparent that, with that advent of digital networks, this balancing act becomes far more precarious. Traditionally, informational works were recorded in physical embodiments such as paper, canvas, and magnetic media, which have mass, weight, and volume. Such media are expensive to transport and distribute. Digital networks drastically lower such costs, allowing nearly costless reproduction and distribution of digitized content. Traditional media also facilitated exclusion, because access to the work could be controlled by controlling access to the embodiment. Such control is far more difficult for digitized works. Thus, computerized networks remove a natural bottleneck that allowed some exclusion quite apart from any legal fence. Digital networks make the disutility of legal exclusion greater, because people could otherwise have the informational good at a marginal cost close to zero; additionally, the networks tend to greatly increase the cost of enforcement, since the ability to copy and distribute the content is now widespread.

Public Goods in Science

The public goods problem addressed by intellectual property law is a problem shared by the scientific community: Indeed, it lies at the heart of the scientific endeavor (Merges, 1996). Books, articles, research protocols, software, databases, and other products of research all require a considerable investment of time and ingenuity to create. However, once created, they are fairly easy to replicate. Thus, science is also in the business of generating valuable information but does so using entirely different methods from those contemplated by the law of intellectual property. Rather than a set of formal rules or legal institutions designed to encourage creativity, science uses informal and often unwritten communal norms to achieve its goals.

The primary norms of the scientific community, as identified in the pioneering work of sociologist Robert Merton, include *universalism*, the expectation that scientists should judge empirical claims according to impersonal criteria, without regard to the identity of their author; *disinterestedness*, the expectation that scientists will subordinate their own biases and interests to the advancement of knowledge; *communalism*, the expectation that discoveries will be freely shared and dedicated to the community of scientists; and *organized skepticism*, the expectation that scientists will subject empirical claims to systematic scrutiny and validation.

These norms function together to drive the scientific enterprise, creating community behavior that rewards contributions to the corpus of scientific information. Scientists are expected to freely contribute their discoveries to the community; such contributed knowledge is vetted through criticism and peer review of published papers or reports. Thus, publication enstanciates both values of communalism and organized skepticism. Contributed knowledge that passes such scrutiny gains the contributor the recognition and respect of his or her peers. Under the norm of universalism, any knowledge contributor can expect to receive such recognition, regardless of social status; the norm of disinterestedness discourages fabrication of knowledge to gain undeserved recognition.

Thus, both the ethos of science and the policy rationale for intellectual property assumes the necessity of an incentive to produce valuable information: However, in contrast to the commercial ethic undergirding intellectual property law, scientific norms rely on reputational rewards as their primary incentive. In most developed nations, this Mertonian ethic is supplemented by heavy governmental subsidization in the form of competitive grants or state-sponsored research positions. The presence of this subsidization and reputational reward incentive at least partially removes the rationale for an intellectual property incentive in scientific research. Scientific norms assume, however, that scientists do not need a pecuniary incentive to engage in creative work; scientists already have a creation incentive in the form of peer recognition.

Indeed, under a Mertonian ethic, intellectual property rights may clash with the scientific values: Legal fences by their nature restrict access to information, contrary to the communal norms of science. Because intellectual property law offers its pecuniary incentive by restricting access to the creative work, assertion of an intellectual property right may violate the scientific norm of communality. Patents, copyrights, and similar proprietary interests may therefore be viewed by scientists as unnecessary at best, and counterproductive at worst. Scientists who seek commercial rewards at the expense of reputational rewards, or who seek both simultaneously, may be viewed by their peers as having "sold out." As suggested above, this problem is most apparent in the category of trade secrecy protection, which can only be maintained so long as the proprietary information remains publicly undisclosed.

Similarly, the scientific communal norm may tend to clash with the substantive legal requirements of patent law, which in most of the world entails a standard of novelty requiring that an invention remain undisclosed to the public prior to the filing of a patent application. Scientists who seek patent protection are less likely to publish promptly, for fear of losing the right to a patent. Additionally, assertion of the patent right, especially by commercial firms, will inevitably block some use of the patented invention by scientists who cannot afford the price of a license for the invention. In its most extreme form, the patent right could even be used to block research that might compete with that of the patent holder—a most serious violation of the Mertonian norms of disinterestedness and communality (Eisenberg, 1994).

This conflict has long been apparent in the situation of industrial researchers, who will generally be drawn from an academic research background, but who will be subject to the proprietary restraints of their industrial employer. In order to attract the best researchers from academic settings, employers may attempt to replicate the conditions of academic research insofar as possible. Many such researchers and the firms that employ them have attempted to walk a precarious line between the rewards of science and those of law; the employer will permit publication of significant research, but only subject to prepublication review to ensure maintenance of the employer's patent and trade secret position. The exercise of corporate censorship and publication veto power necessary to maintain the employer's intellectual property portfolio has frequently made this hybrid arrangement a frustrating exercise for both employer and employee.

This tension has been analyzed at some length by Eisenberg (1987), who has traced the commercialization of scientific knowledge in the context of biotechnology research. The potential for commercialization of many genes, proteins, or other biotechnology discoveries creates an incentive contrary to the communal norm of science, leading some scientists to withhold research samples from others who purportedly wished to replicate or extend published research. As a result, some scientific journals have gone so far as to require that researchers agree to make available materials discussed in accepted papers before the journal will agree to publish the paper. Similar controversies have also arisen with regard to the propriety of patenting protein or nucleic acid sequences determined as part of the Human Genome Mapping and Sequencing initiatives; although some believe that the availability of patents will spur research on these projects, many in the scientific community have loudly denounced proprietary claims on what they believe to be the common property of all scientists.

Cyberspace Norms

Commercial biotechnology is by no means the only arena in which commercial and scientific norms have come into conflict. Similar tensions can be seen in the development of the present Global Information Infrastructure, or "information superhighway" from the Internet. The history of the Internet is largely the history of electronic research collaboration from its earliest days as ARPAnet, a Department of Defense (DoD) research project (Giese, 1996). The network and its development were subsequently entrusted to the custody of the National Science Foundation, and the users during this critical period of the network's growth were not primarily soldiers or military personnel, but members of the NSF sponsored scientific research community. Only relatively recently has the network been "privatized" for public and commercial usage.

Thus, the early history of the network was dominated by academic research usage and academic users, both in computer science and in other areas of basic research. Historians of the net have described in some detail how the "hacker ethic" of ARPAnet designers clashed with the values and expectations of the United States Department of Defense, which supplied funding for the project. This hacker ethic, which to some extent continues today in Internet culture, emphasizes sharing of resources and unrestricted informational flows, an ethic consistent with the scientific norms of communalism. The conventions of Internet usage, or *nettiquette* appear also to reflect these norms—thus, acceptable network custom discourages waste of bandwidth, discourages reliance on title or status, and reputationally rewards contribution of resources . On occasion, these conventions have even been raised to the status of formal rules, as when during the years of NSF oversight, prohibitions against commercial traffic on the network backbone were a formal part of the network's Acceptable Use Policy (AUP).

But perhaps more important than the legacy of behavioral conventions on the Internet is the signature that its early designers left embedded in its technology. Commentators on the Internet have observed that in contrast to the rigid command military structure one might have expected of a Department of Defense research project, the decentralized and nonhierarchical structure of the Internet appears to embody the distinctly nonhierarchical attitudes of the researchers employed by the military. This architecture in turn lent itself to usage outside the uses envisioned by the DoD, but which were quite in keeping with the attitudes of the network's academic designers and users. This open technological approach was continued under the auspices of the NSF, as one might expect of users steeped in the communal norms of science.

Thus, the technological characteristics of the network appears to bear out the general rule that artifacts reflect the values of their users. Scholars studying the history and sociological impact of technology have long argued that technologies embody the values of their creators, and the values thus embodied may include social values otherwise unassociated with the artifact itself. This concept is by itself hardly surprising, as in one aspect it forms the basis for the study of the humanities; we assume that the characteristics of an artifact can tell us something about the thoughts and culture of the artifact's creators, and technological artifacts yield such clues in the same manner as architecture or art. Some care must be taken in drawing such inferences, as some artifactual characteristics may not necessarily embody value choices. Many design choices will be the result of manufacturing or marketing constraints, although of course even such utilitarian design choices assume certain values, and the technological embodiment of such values through artifacts is not socially trivial. But many other technological design choices are not necessarily choices about durability, manufacturing cost, or consumer appeal, and may more clearly reflect the value choices of the technology's builders and users.

We may therefore perceive echoes of the Internet's research heyday in its current function and design. In general, the network is superbly suited to facilitate information exchange, and to resist geographic, cultural, or legal impediments to the free flow of information. The network is structured to enable remote access and resource sharing, as might be expected of technology embodying norms of communality; it affords few clues as to the identity or status of users, as might be expected of technology embodying norms of universality and disinterestedness; it disseminates information according to a nonhierarchical and decentralized structure, as again might be expected of technology embodying norms of universality and communality.

This type of open network architecture may be desirable and even necessary for shared resources in an environment where the incentive structure for innovation relies primarily on reputational reward. But when the network is put to uses other than those assumed by its creators, as Internet now has been, the assumptions embedded in the technology may create conflicts. Many of the current legal controversies related to the Internet appear to be grounded in the disjunction between the network's embodiment of scientific norms, and current commercial usages that assume entirely different values. Ongoing social disputes have arisen from the inability of legal restrictions to effectively control content in a medium that not only rapidly reproduces and disseminates content, but also lacks any central control point or organizational hierarchy from which to restrict such dissemination. Thus, to name only two examples that bracket the debate over digitized content, the widespread availability of pornographic content on the Internet, including availability to underage users, stems in large measure from the network's open character (Weinberg, 1997), as does the debate over unauthorized reproduction and dissemination of copyrighted content.

However, what technology can impart, it can also restrict. Legal controversies involving the Internet have been increasingly linked to technological proposals that may be viewed as an attempt to build back into the network constraints or limitations that its designers purposefully avoided. This may in some cases be accomplished by the application of legal regimes to fence out objectionable content, or to fence in valuable content. Alternatively, the same result may be sought by constructing technological fences. In the case of online pornography, automated filters or "censorware" are being considered to screen out content that may be inappropriate for minors. In the case of intellectual property, cryptographic "lock out" programs have been designed to deny unauthorized users access to digitized content that the net makes freely available.

This technological approach to legal problems, which Joel Reidenberg has called *lex informatica*, or governance through technology, may largely obviate the need for explicit legal standards: The technology can be purposefully designed to instantiate the desired behavior (Reidenberg, 1998). But such an approach raises the prospect of what Lawrence Lessig has dubbed "tyranny in the infrastructure," in essence the dark side of technological constraints on behavior (Lessig, 1997). Legal fences are relatively porous or "leaky," allowing some level of infringement to go undetected or unpunished. In the case of intellectual property, such a practical tolerance for infringement represents a loss of rights and revenue for intellectual property owners, but may provide important flexibility to the overall legal system—perhaps by allowing, for example, minor copyright or patent infringements that facilitate research or enhance personal learning. By contrast, technological fences may be far less yielding, deterring all infractions because within the system, such an infraction is simply impossible. Intellectual property owners gain rights and revenue, but at the cost of the former flexibility and its incremental benefits.

Given the impetus toward such technological governance, the tension between the values of science and those of intellectual property law takes on an added dimension for the design of collaborative research technologies. If the Internet embodies design choices at odds with information control, future architectures will be amenable to the same choices, and designers of technology for future collaborative research will face much the same quandary now apparent in the value-based disputes over Internet usage. Researchers in collaboratory projects must therefore be cognizant of the assumptions built into the collaborative system. The very nature of collaborative electronic interaction entails the likelihood of shared data files, system access by multiple users, and other features of a reflective of an open architecture network. To the extent that the system design further embodies communal or universal notions of scientific collaboration, the features of the system itself may tend to defeat or complicate the ability to protect the fruits of the collaboration via intellectual property mechanisms (Gould, 1989). Thus, technology that lends itself to collaborative research will tend toward an open architecture and reflect communal norms, whereas technology that fosters intellectual property rights will tend to hamper data sharing, information transfer, and remote equipment access.

Digital Copyright

Where digital media are concerned, copyright issues are plentiful and often intractable, because of the operation of the technology. These qualifications for copyright protection, which were developed in the world of print media, do not always map well onto the world of digital media, particularly in a networked environment. In a very real sense, digital networks are designed to function via reproduction and distribution of digitized materials. Thus, a pivotal question in the analysis of copyright in digital media is the issue of so-called "RAM copies" (Hardy, 1997). In automated information processing and retrieval systems, digitized information is reproduced and stored in computer memory whenever the information is accessed. For example, this storage may occur in RAM, or it may occur in temporary "cache" files on magnetic media. In the case of networked computer communications, temporary copies may be made on several intermediate machines as packets are routed to their final destination.

Some courts have suggested that copies of a program loaded into RAM may be relevant for copyright purposes. Because the RAM copies are accessible and endure for more than a transitory duration, these decisions hold that the copy in RAM may be an infringing copy. This in turn implies that intermediate copies, including browser caches, that are created during the operation of network applications, may be infringing copies. In turn, digital transmission of those copies over a network would presumably constitute a distribution of copies. To the extent that such reproduction and distribution is unauthorized, this implies that the normal operation of computers and computer networks results in repeated and widespread copyright infringement (Litman, 1994).

Such reasoning is controversial and has been criticized by many scholars (Jaszi, 1996; McManis, 1996; Samuelsen, 1996). Others have observed that even if one accepts the idea that RAM copies are relevant for copyright purposes, at least two theories exist to ameliorate the potential effects of this holding (Lemley, 1994). These theories fall under the respective rubrics of implied license and fair use. Implied licenses are contractual agreements that, although not written or formally negotiated, are inferred from the actions of two parties. Fair use encompasses a body of copyright law that permits certain socially necessary uses of copyrighted works, which would otherwise infringe the exclusive rights of the owner. For example, U.S. courts have held that a copy of computer software made incidentally in the course of reverse engineering uncopyrightable portions of the software is permissible as a fair use.

Drawing on a theory of implied license, we might infer that the generation of RAM copies in a computer network is permitted under the terms of an unwritten contract for use of materials on a public network. Or, in the alternative, we might conclude that the creation of such copies is a fair use of the work. Either conclusion stems from the placement of the work in digital form onto a networked system. By placing the material on an open network, the owner must have intended that RAM copies be made and distributed, that digital transmissions occur. We conclude that there is some implied license for those actions to transpire as the material is accessed. Alternatively, under a fair use theory, we infer that the occurrence of such reproduction, distribution, performance, and display as occurs in digital transmission is a fair use of the work that occurs in the course of accessing it in the manner that the author apparently intended it to be accessed. If the owner of the work did not intend the work to be copied, distributed, performed, and displayed, he or she could well have restricted access to the material.

Copyright In References

The poor fit between past conception of intellectual property and use of digital media is nowhere more apparent than in the growing conflict over hypermedia. Explosive expansion of hypermedia usage, particularly via the Internet, has prompted the filing of at least three lawsuits involving the issue of unsolicited hyperlinking (O'Rourke, 1998). Plaintiffs in these cases have alleged that hyperlinks referencing material at other sites on the World Wide Web infringe intellectual property rights in referenced material. In particular, infringement of copyright, trademark, and related business reputation rights have been claimed. Such legal claims have important ramifications for hypermedia: If the infringement claims are legally valid, development and use of hypermedia works may be curtailed by legal liability.

The gravamen of the copyright claims in particular has been that the supplier of the reference either infringes the copyright in the referenced materials, or assists others to infringe the copyright in the referenced material. In the case of hypertext, one possible theory of direct copyright infringement might be to assert that the reference used in the hypertext link is itself the subject of copyright, and so the creator of a link who uses the reference without permission is engaged in infringement. However, recent court decisions have held that facts generally, and reference citations in particular, do not constitute copyrightable subject matter. A similar result would be expected with regard to hypertext linkages; a URL is essentially a location or identification number referencing a file somewhere on the Internet. Considered as a location, it seems unlikely that the URL can be subject to copyright protection by anyone, let alone the author or owner of the material referenced by the URL. Because it is in essence an address, the reference is not the proper subject of copyright: It is simply an indicator of location, which is to say, a fact. If the reference is not copyrightable, then inclusion of it in a document cannot be infringement.

If use of the URL or reference is not itself a source of infringement, then might its employment in retrieving the referenced document constitute infringement? Because the referenced document is loaded when the link is activated, it may appear to the user of the link that the supplier of the link is also supplying the referenced material without authorization of the material's owner. However, at an operational level, it is extremely difficult to see how the hyperlink offeror might have directly infringed the exclusive rights of the owner of the material. Even if we accept the theory that RAM copies are relevant for purposes of copyright, no copy is ever made on the hyperlink site server (Cavazos & Miles, 1997). Rather, the user's computer takes the URL reference from the site and uses that information to request copies from the site where the copyrighted material is resident. Copies might be made as the material is transferred from its resident site to the user's computer. But these copies neither originate from, nor pass through the site where the hyperlink is found. The seamless transition from the initial site to the site referenced is merely an illusion of the interface as seen by the user.

This analysis holds whether the link involved is manually activated—by pointing to and clicking on highlighted text or buttons in the interface—or whether the link is automatic, as is the usual case for displayed images using the HTML "IMG" code. Although in one instance the referenced material is called up at the user's discretion, and in the other it is called up automatically, in neither case does the creator of the link copy, distribute, perform, or display the referenced material. The same is true whether the referenced material is displayed "inline" or not. The analysis similarly holds whether considered as a matter of reproduction and distribution of copies, or whether as a matter of public performance and display. Any copies made or transmissions performed originate from the server where the material is housed.

Although copyright claims of this sort appear to have little legal merit, they continue to be asserted because of the future stakes in controlling valuable information. Such claims could potentially chill the independent development of hypertext networks, placing development within the control of content owners. Additionally, were such claims to be found valid, they could form the basis for proprietary control of information tagging and reference. The hypertext link is in essence an automated version of a scholarly footnote or bibliographic reference: it tells the reader where to find the referenced material. In the case of hypertext, the user's browser or other application can then retrieve the material from its location, a process that is not only hidden from the user, but far more convenient than physically venturing into library stacks to retrieve hardcopy referenced in a plain footnote. These cases therefore have broad ramifications for scholarly citation, bibliographic indexing, and information cataloging (Burk, 1998). And, in an environment where lookup and retrieval of the referenced work is automated, the cases have similarly broad ramifications for information access. In the emerging world of information technology, control of information references may be tantamount to control of information access.

Database Protection

The efforts to control information indexes through copyright claims, described above, underscore the value of data compilations in the coming information economy. The orderly selection and arrangement of data has long been central to the practice of science, but commercial creation and exploitation of databases not only for scientific research, but for education, finance, marketing, entertainment and other purposes now comprises a substantial service sector. Publishers of such databases will be seeking commercial rewards, rather than reputational rewards, for the time and effort required to compile and arrange such data. Even noncommercial researchers will find themselves under increasing pressure to hold their data compilations proprietary, or risk seeing their efforts captured and incorporated into commercial databases.

However, the scope of proprietary rights in data or data compilations may be uncertain under current law. Copyright law provides some protection against unauthorized reproduction of certain compilations, but this protection is limited to original compilations and in no event extends to the compiled data itself. These limitations are perhaps best illustrated in the landmark case of *Feist v. Rural Telephone and Telegraph*, a lawsuit over copyright infringement of telephone directory white pages. In *Feist*, the Supreme Court of the United States held that there could be no infringement from copying such a compilation, because the directory contained no copyrightable expression. No copyright could apply to the individual items in the directory, because names, addresses, and telephone numbers are simply unprotectable facts. Furthermore, the court reasoned, there are essentially only two viable ways to arrange such facts in a directory: by name in alphabetical order, or numerically in the type of directory used by telemarketers. Choosing one of those two arrangements—alphabetical arrangement—failed the requirement for originality, and so the telephone directory was ineligible for copyright protection, and could be freely copied.

Because of the *Feist* holding, and similar conclusions reached by courts in the United Kingdom and Canada, many types of data compilations fail to qualify for any meaningful intellectual property protection. Those compilations that follow a routine but useful scheme of selection and arrangement will be unprotectable by copyright, even if they are fairly expensive to produce. Some such compilations may receive limited protection in the United States under state misappropriation laws; some courts have suggested that taking another publisher's "hot news" for commercial gain constitutes an unfair trade practice. However, this approach to database protection is questionable in light of the *Feist* decision, and is in any event limited to facts of a short durational value, such as stock quotes. There is also some indication in recent cases that data structures or informational hierarchies stored in machine memory may be patentable. However, in order to be patentable, such arrangements must meet the high patentability standards of nonobviousness, utility, and novelty; therefore, as a practical matter, patent may be even less available than copyright as a form of database protection. Some types of compilations might be maintained as trade secrets, but as a practical matter it will be difficult to both commercially exploit a data compilation and maintain the level of confidentiality necessary for trade secrecy.

In the absence of any strong protection from copyright, patent, or other existing categories of intellectual property, database publishers have lobbied hard in the U.S. Congress for legislation granting proprietary rights in collections of information (Reichman & Samuelson, 1997). Such legislation would in essence create a brand new form of intellectual property, separate from any protection afforded by other proprietary rights, and including subject matter that would be unprotectable by copyright, patent, or trade secrecy (Ginsburg, 1997). The proposed statute would not protect individual items of data, but would protect an extremely broad category of "collections of information" if created by substantial effort or commercial investment. Unauthorized extraction of any "substantial" portion of a database would be prohibited, although what might constitute a substantial portion is unclear.

Because of ambiguities in crucial terms such as *substantial*, the legislation has been vigorously opposed by a variety of scientific organizations, including the National Academy of Sciences and the American Association for the Advancement of Science. These critics of the proposal charge that it would drastically limit competition among commercial database providers, raise the cost of access to commercial databases, and frustrate research using compilations of information. In response, advocates for database protection included in the proposed statute an exemption for use of databases in scientific research. However, the exemption would be limited to scientific use that does not "harm" the "actual or potential market" for the database. This proposal has failed to satisfy critics of the database legislation because the exemption appears to be largely illusory, because any use of a database without full payment could be said to "harm the market" for that compilation. It is difficult to imagine when if ever researchers could rely on the exemption.

The concerns of public interest and scientific organizations ultimately frustrated passage of the database legislation during the 105th Congress. However, the same proposal is likely to be reintroduced in the 106th Congress and eventually enacted in some form. Much of the continued agitation for such legislation in the United States stems from the promulgation of a European Union (EU) directive that requires EU member nations to adopt precisely such database protection. Under the European database directive EU nations must enact database protection that, like the proposed U.S. legislation, grants new proprietary rights in a broad range of both electronic and nonelectronic collections of material created through a substantial investment of time and money. The proprietary rights include use or extraction of a substantial portion of such collections for 15 years; a new 15 years begins each time the database is added to. Most importantly, the EU directive contains a requirement of international reciprocity; that is, this new type of protection will be granted to data compilations from nonmember states only if the originating state has similar provisions available to protect EU compilations. Thus, if U.S. database publishers are to receive database protection under these European laws, the United States must have similar laws in place. U.S. database publishers have therefore lobbied hard for the enactment of such U.S. database legislation.

Contract Law

Although databases may fail to qualify for intellectual property protection against the public at large, content owners may attempt to achieve a similar scope of protection via contract, by premising access to the desired informational goods on acceptance of restrictive terms. Such attempts to extend proprietary rights have become commonplace in the software industry, which has long styled the purchase of software as a license or rental agreement. This practice began as a convenient fiction for software publishers to avoid the copyright First Sale doctrine. Under the First Sale doctrine, once a copy is sold the buyer is free to dispose of the copy as he or she wishes—perhaps giving it away or reselling it in a used product market that competes with sales by the publishers. However if the copy is licensed or rented to the consumer, rather than sold, the First Sale doctrine would not apply to the transaction, and the consumer would have much less latitude in disposing of the copy. Additionally, the producer may also incorporate into the terms of the license other restrictions beyond those he would be entitled to via copyright.

However, unlike a simple sale, a limited license of this sort requires negotiation of terms. Negotiating a licensing contract with every consumer would be extremely onerous, especially for mass-market products where tens of thousands of such negotiations would be required each year. Software publishers have therefore adopted standardized massmarket licenses with nonnegotiable "take it or leave it" terms—the proverbial "fine print" contract. However, under AngloAmerican contract law, one party cannot unilaterally declare terms: Formation of a valid license or contract generally requires an intent by both parties to the contract to be bound by the terms of the terms of that contract. Software publishers have attempted to deal with the requirement of agreement, without separately negotiating every transaction, through the fiction of "manifesting assent," that is, by inferring an agreement from the actions of the purchasing party. This has given rise to the so called "shrinkwrap" license, a legal conceit that assumes the consumer, by opening the packaging of the software, has shown an intent to be bound by the terms of the license governing the software (Lemley 1995). A similar fiction, "clickwrap" or "webwrap" licenses, are said to arise when the consumer clicks an icon or button displayed on the screen. Additionally, this practice has now spread beyond software to other types of informational transactions, such as commercial database or web site access.

This fiction rests on the questionable assumption that the consumer's actions in opening a package or using a product shows intent to be bound to the terms of the accompanying license—but the actions may simply show an intent to use the product. Indeed, it is entirely possible—even likely—that the user has never read or understood the terms of the license to which he or she has supposedly manifested assent. Thus, it is unclear how much credence one can give to the inference that by taking some innocuous action, a consumer has read or understood the terms of the standardized contract offered by the buyer. For example, in the case of classic shrinkwraps, the consumer frequently cannot read the terms of the license until after having opened the packaging—by which time he or she is assumed to have agreed to the terms of the inaccessible license. In the case of "clickwrap" or "webwrap" agreements," it is particularly difficult to determine who may be the clicking the "I agree" icon; the action may be traced to a particular machine that has accessed a web site, but contracts are made with individuals, not machines, and many individuals may use the same machine.

Additionally, sophisticated sellers may take advantage of less sophisticated consumers by obscuring surprising or egregious contract terms in difficult language or by burying such terms the contract's extensive fine print. Most purchasers of software would be extremely surprised to learn that they have supposedly licensed the software they paid for, rather than purchasing it. Other terms in software mass-market licenses may be equally surprising, including purported agreements to copyrightlike restrictions on unprotectable subject matter, such as public domain works or facts; terms stating that the purchaser waives his rights to fair use of the material; or even agreements to allow the copyright holder a stake in products created through use of the licensed information.

As a consequence, courts in the United States have typically declined to enforce "shrinkwrap" agreements, in part because of doubts that any consumer would truly agree to such overreaching terms, and in part because such terms may be considered unconscionable, or contrary to public policy. Additionally, because contract law in the United States is state law, and so subordinate to federal law, contracts may be negated or "preempted" when they attempt to circumvent or violate superior federal policies. Many mass market terms designed to give content owners rights not permitted to them under copyright law may be preempted by the federal statute, or by the Constitution itself (O'Rourke, 1995).

Because shrinkwrap licenses are often unenforceable under current law, content publishers have sought sweeping changes in the Uniform Commercial Code (UCC) that governs contracts in most states. At the time of this writing, the proposed UCC changes have metamorphosized through a variety of drafts, the most recent of which has been named the Uniform Computer Information Transaction Act, or UCITA. But in each of its incarnations, the statute would make enforceable terms to which a consumer had "manifested assent," even surprising or egregiously unfair terms. Additionally, the proposed changes would apply not simply to software, but would apply to all transactions in "computer information." Although these changes could be partially preempted by federal law, such changes in contract law could provide content publishers with a powerful tool to control terms of access to information in the 21st century (Lemley, 1999).

The proliferation of "clickwrap" agreements in electronic commerce carries with it the likelihood that many aspects of scientific research will be increasingly subjected to such contracts. Researchers and research institutions will be confronted with these agreements in order to gain access to commercial databases, commercially produced software applications, or other proprietary digital works. Yet even setting aside such encounters with commercial licensing, scientists will likely see such contracts applied to noncommercial information related to collaborative research. Collaboration will necessarily require sharing of data and access to collaborator's files. The international problem alluded to at the beginning of this chapter adds additional complexity to the problem, because it will be difficult to determine the applicable law in the event of a dispute. Electronic collaborators may attempt to address these problems via standardized agreements that will require some manifestation of assent before shared files or "collaboratory" space can be accessed; the contracts may specify the obligations of collaborators, dictate the permissible usage of shared information, or designate the law that may apply in the event of disputes.

A form of such standardized agreements has already become relatively common in biotechnology, where a "letters license" may accompany materials transfers; the agreement, much like a type of "shrinkwrap," may attempt to impose on the recipient obligations not to further share the materials, or attempt to restrict dissemination of experimental results obtained by using the materials, or may even purport grant the materials donor a share in any valuable discoveries arising from use of the materials (Burk, 1994a). Such requirements have been somewhat controversial, as their terms may not be fully compatible with the norms of science. The research community will face difficulty choices in deciding whether this approach to proprietary rights management will be allowed to further proliferate in electronic collaborations (Burk, 1997).

Technological Fences

The emergence of boilerplate contracts as a preferred tool for controlling commercial access to digital works rests in part on development of technological restrictions on information. Some type of restriction on content access is a critical adjunct to the use of "clickwrap" contracts: If access to information is to be premised on acceptance of certain licensing terms, then access must somehow be denied unless the terms are accepted. As we have seen, intellectual property rights serve to some extent to restrict access to information, by providing a legal deterrent to unauthorized uses of protected material. But unlike physical access restrictions, legal "fences" are relatively leaky; they offer only behavioral incentives that may not always be sufficient to deter unauthorized access. The effectiveness of legal deterrence is only as great as the owner's ability to detect unauthorized access, monitor use, and enforce her rights. Additionally, legal for some types of content, such as databases, copyright and other intellectual property regimes may be inapplicable, even though the creator of the content would like to restrict access.

Software or hardware "lock out" controls, commonly referred to as *copyright management systems* (CMS), may therefore be employed to supply what intellectual property law cannot (Cohen, 1995). Such software "lockout" systems would use sophisticated cryptographic algorithms to prevent access to their associated content without a proper password or decryption key. Before accessing such encrypted information, a user would be required to contact the information owner to receive the key—presumably in return for payment. Thus, digitized information, including software, text, graphics, and data could in this fashion be electronically fenced off from unauthorized access. Sophisticated management systems could also be used to prevent copying of digitized information after it had been accessed: Thus, use of the information could be limited to an agreed on period or agreed on form of usage (Stefik, 1996).

Additionally, CMS may be employed to solve the owner's monitoring and detection needs. Technology is also becoming available in a networked environment to combine such lockout systems with identification and micropayment systems to create what one commentator has dubbed "books that rat on you." Such copyright management systems would not only notify the information owner when the information was accessed, but would monitor usage of the information, charging the user per copy, per minute of access, per word, or per bit.

On closer consideration, it is clear that the title of "copyright management system" may be something of a misnomer, as this application of this *lex informatica* approach essentially eliminates the rationale for copyright law. Information that has been fenced off via copyright management software is no longer nonexclusive because the system excludes unauthorized uses, turning a public good into a private good. The application of such technological fences may also extend beyond informational works subject to copyright. Any information, even that which is unprotectable or in the public domain, could potentially be fenced off in this manner. Thus, copyright protection for the content becomes irrelevant because copying is impossible unless the protective technology is circumvented. To the extent that CMS users require legal protection, it will be protection against unauthorized "hacking" of their CMS system, and in the United States, such laws have been enacted with the 1998 Digital Millennium Copyright Act, which penalizes circumvention of technological "lockout" systems.

One disturbing aspect of a CMS regime, especially when backed by legal sanction for circumvention, is the rigidity of control over protected information (Cohen, 1996). Unlike legal fences, such technological fences are unforgiving to all unauthorized access, including legally permissible unauthorized uses, such as fair use. Indeed, CMS renders the public incapable of making fair use of content because they will be technologically precluded from doing so.

This effective elimination of fair use in digital media is a matter of little concern to those who conceptualize fair use as a necessary evil, an intrusion on copyright that has previously been tolerated only because tracking and negotiating for small uses of copyrighted material was too costly (Bell, 1998). Some argue that fair use has existed only because the cost of the negotiation over small snippets of copyrighted material would be greater than the value of the use, and so the use would never occur. Rather than deterring such small incursions on the copyright, the user was permitted to help himself to what would otherwise be infringing quotes and snippets of the material. Under this conception of fair use, some content owners argue that fair use is no longer necessary in an environment of micropayments, because even the smallest usages of copyrighted material can be monitored, valued, and paid for (Stefik, 1997).

In contrast, other commentators have argued that public rights including fair use should remain viable even in an environment where minimal uses can be commodified (Cohen, 1967). This alternative conception of intellectual property views rights such as fair use as important accommodations between values of democratic free inquiry and the restrictions imposed by copyright. Under this view, regardless of any technological ability to track every use of digitized information, the public should still not need to seek permission for some uses of creative works—for example, in cases where a scholar or reviewer intends to engage in criticism of a work, for which a content holder might never give permission. And of course, such critical review is clearly integral to the organized skepticism function of science.

In an era of copyright management systems, rights of public use in turn necessarily imply some right of public access because the ability to make fair use of content is meaningless if is blocked by technological "lock out" devices from obtaining the content. The assertion of such rights of access is a novel legal issue, as publication of information in previous media has always entailed public access—indeed, the point of intellectual property law was to moderate such public access. Only in emerging digital media does a publisher have the option of both publicly distributing content while simultaneously restricting access to it. As was observed above with regard to trade secrecy, widespread restriction of access to data, whether via physical containment or technological containment, hampers peer review and other core scientific institutions that requires unfettered access to research data. Thus, the proliferation of technological fences may threaten not only electronic collaboration , but the scientific enterprise itself.

CONCLUSION

Intellectual property law has gained increasing importance in networked environments due to the perceived need for commercial publishers to hold digitized information proprietary. At the same time, the recent history of basic research has been characterized by an increasing tension between values of scientific communality and commercial proprietary interests. Discussion of scientific values has been punctuated by debates over the commercialization of information, and the acceptability of restraining information through the legal mechanisms of patents, copyrights, or trade secrecy. This same tension may be both implicitly and explicitly expressed in the technological architecture networked environments; digital format has can enhance the accessibility and dissemination of information, whereas technological "lock out" devices can be used to sequester information for commercial gain. In networked digital environments, legal constraints and technological constraints may be interchangeable or even complementary in holding information proprietary. Thus, researchers in electronic collaborations, who will be working at the intersection of these social policy debates, can expect to be faced with increasingly difficult choices as to the degree of openness or constraint of information accessibility in such collaborations.

REFERENCES

Bell, T. W. (1998). Fair use vs. fared use: The impact of automated rights management on copyright's Fair Use Doctrine. *North Carolina Law Review, 76,* 558.

Burk, D. L. (1993). Patents in cyberspace: Territoriality and infringement on global computer networks. *Tulane Law Review, 68,* 1.

Burk, D. L. (1994a). Misappropriation of trade secrets in biotechnology licensing. *Albany Law Journal of Science & Technology, 4,* 121.

Burk, D. L. (1994b). Transborder intellectual property issues on the electronic frontier. *Stanford Law & Policy Review, 5,* 9.

Burk, D. L. (1997). Challenges to copyright law and fair use by new information technology. In A. Teich, S. Nelson, & C. McEnaney (Eds.), *AAAS Science Yearbook.*

Burk, D. L. (1998). Proprietary rights in hypertext linkages. *Journal of Information Law and Technology.* <http://elj.warwick.ac.uk/jilt/intprop/98_2burk/>

Cavazos, E. A. , & Miles, C. F. (1997). Copyright on the WWW. Linking and liability. *Richmond Journal of Law & Technology, (4)*3. <http://www.richmond.edu/~jolt/v4i2/cavazos.html>

Cohen, J. (1997). Some reflections on copyright management systems and laws designed to protect them. *Berkeley Technology Law Journal, 12,* 161.

Cohen, J. E. (1995). Reverse engineering and the rise of electronic vigilantism: Intellectual property implications of "Lock-Out" programs. *Southern California Law Review, 68,* 1091.

Cohen, J. E. (1996). A Right to read anonymously: A closer look at copyright management in cyberspace. *Connecticut Law Review, 28,* 981.

Eisenberg, R. (1987). Proprietary rights and the norms of science in biotechnology research. *Yale Law Journal, 97,* 177.

Eisenberg, R. (1994). Technology transfer and the genome project: Problems with patenting research tools. *Risk: Health, Safety, & Environment, 5,* 163.

Geller, P. E. (1996). Conflicts of law in cyberspace: International copyright in a digitally networked world. In B. Hugenholz (Ed.), *The future of copyright in a digital environment* (p. 27). The Hague, London, Boston: Kluwer Law International.

Giese, M. (1996). From ARPAnet to the internet: A cultural clash and its implications in framing the debate on the information superhighway. In L. Strate et al. (Eds.), *Communication and cyberspace: Social interaction in an electronic environment* (p. 123). The Hague, Boston: Kluwer Law International.

Ginsburg, J. C. (1995). Global use/territorial rights: Private international law questions about the global information infrastructure. *Journal of Copyright Sociology, 42,* 318.

Ginsburg, J. C. (1997). Copyright, common law, and sui generis protection of databases in the United States and abroad. *University of Cincinnati Law Review, 57,* 151.

Gould, C. C. (1989). Network ethics: Access, consent, and the informed community. In C. Gould (Ed.), *The information web: Ethical and social implications of computer networking* (p. 1). Boulder, CO: Westview Press.

Hardy, I. T. (1997). Computer RAM copies: Hit or myth? Historical perspectives on caching as a microcosm of current copyright concerns. *University of Dayton Law Review, 22,* 548.

Jaszi, P. (1996). Caught in the net of copyright. *Oregon Law Review, 75,* 277.

Lemley, M. A. (1995). Intellectual property and shrinkwrap licenses. *Southern California Law Review, 68,* 1239.

Lemley, M. A. (1997). Dealing with overlapping copyrights on the internet. *University of Dayton Law Review, 22,* 548.

Lemley, M. A. (1999). Beyond preemption: The law and policy of intellectual property licensing. *California Law Review, 87,* 111.

Lessig, L. (1997) Tyranny in the infrastructure. *Wired, 5*(7), 96.

Litman, J. (1994). The exclusive right to read. *Cardozo Arts and Entertainment Law Journal, 13,* 29.

McManis, C. R. (1996). Taking TRIPS on the information superhighway: International intellectual property protection and emerging computer technology. *Villanova Law Review, 41,* 207.

Merges, R. P. (1996). Property rights theory and the commons: The case of scientific research. *Social Philosophy & Policy, 145.*

O'Rourke, M. A. (1995). Drawing the boundary between copyright and contract: Copyright preemption of software license terms. *Duke Law Journal, 45,* 479.

O'Rourke, M. A. (1998). Fencing cyberspace: Drawing borders in a virtual world. *Minnesota Law Review, 82,* 609, 611–612.

Reichman, J. H., & Samuelson, P. (1997). Intellectual property rights in data? *Vanderbilt Law Review, 50.*

Reidenberg, J. (1998). Lex Informatica. *Texas Law Review, 76,* 553.

Samuelson, P. (1996). The copyright grab. *Wired, 4*(1), 134.

Stefik, M. (1996). Letting loose the light: Igniting commerce in electronic publication. In M. Stefik (Ed.), *Internet dreams: Archetypes, myths, and metaphors* (p. 219). MIT Press: Cambridge, MA.

Stefik, M. (1997). Shifting the possible: How digital property rights challenge us to re-think digital publishing. *Berkeley Technology Law Journal, 12,* 138.

Weinberg, J. (1997). Rating the net. *Hastings Communication and Entertainment Journal, 19,* 453.

3 Federated Database Technology for Data Integration: Lessons From Bioinformatics

Peter M. D. Gray
Graham J. L. Kemp
University of Aberdeen

Neuroinformatics can learn much from bioinformatics, particularly the database developments for protein structure and genome data. Here people gradually are learning the discipline of a database schema for data validation and sharing and evolution of data description.

We argue the need for a federated information infrastructure that gives interoperability between sites, as described and advocated for protein and genome data by Robbins (1995). The crisis of integration cannot be met by copying and consolidation because the number of resources is large and growing. Instead we need a collection of resources that is perceived by users to be functionally integrated, yet it maintains its autonomy.

There are various ways to do this based on computing science research, but the crucial issue is the provision of a common semantics and a Shared Data Model, so that data with different meaning are not mistakenly combined, and that data combined from autonomous sources satisfy integrity constraints. This is provided in advanced database systems such as Object-Relational systems and object databases using Semantic Data Models. It is not provided by WWW, but could be provided by web interfaces to loosely coupled federated autonomous databases, sharing an extensible data model. We describe the problems involved in developing such a model, and describe a system built using a mediator that follows these principles.

INTRODUCTION

Bioinformatics and neuroinformatics are data-rich areas where the ability to correlate different kinds of data from different sources can bring additional benefits. *Bioinformatics* does not have an agreed definition, but that given by Robbins (1995) is helpful. He stated that it "refers to database-like activities involving persistent sets of biological data that are maintained in a consistent state over essentially indefinite periods of time." Some also use the term bioinformatics more widely to refer to algorithmic tools commonly used in computational biology or even the infrastructure of communication networks used to support computer-based biological analyses, but in this paper we concentrate on its database management problems and draw lessons from our own work, and experiences of others that should be of relevance in neuroinformatics.

Bioinformatics resources are growing rapidly in size and in number. Early data collections were typically independent collections of formatted text files distributed periodically on magnetic tape or, later, CD ROMs from a central repository. Many data collections are now mirrored at various sites worldwide and many are accessible via the World Wide Web (WWW or Web). Although the internet has reduced the problems of data distribution, data curation is an increasing demanding activity, with centers devoted to maintaining data collections (e.g., protein structure data at Brookhaven National Laboratory and genome sequence data at the European Bioinformatics Institute). This growth has taken place over the last 20 years, and it looks as though neuroinformatics may follow suit.

Many different file and database management systems are currently in use with biological data sets. Many widely used databanks consist of readable flat files of data—each databank containing a different kind of data, and each having its own format for its entries. Some biological data are held in relational databases, for example, the BIPED (Islam & Sternberg, 1989) and SESAM (Huysmans, Richelle, & Wodak, 1991) projects both used commercial database management systems with protein structure data. Object models are gaining in popularity in the genome community—the Object-Protocol Model (OPM, Chen & Markowitz, 1995) and the ACEDB model (Durbin & Thierry-Mieg, 1992) are widely used with various specialized collections of genome data.

There are several reasons why this heterogeneity has arisen. For example, experimental scientists are usually the custodians of these data collections and they are likely to use whatever tools were known and available to them. They may choose a simple physical representation to make porting and exchanging data easy. A more significant reason is that certain physical representations are more appropriate than others for particular kinds of data, and are better suited to the kinds of searches performed against those data. Frequently a great deal of effort goes into developing customized search engines to answer particular kinds of query efficiently, and in developing graphical interfaces tailored to the application. We should like to take advantage of this earlier investment by making use of existing search engines whenever possible.

Bioinformatics faces a "crisis of data integration" (Robbins, 1995), which is compounded by heterogeneity. Ideally, users should be able to access these diverse resources in a uniform way (Fig. 3.1). In addressing this, we advocate the use of a strong semantic data model to describe the data held in data resources, and believe this to be essential for integrating data from different sources. Although some online resources have hypertext links from one databank entry to related entries in other databanks, the WWW does not provide a sufficient style of access as users become more demanding in their data requests. Nor does it facilitate automatic interrogation by programs.

In this chapter, we first consider the characteristics of data collections in biological and neurological fields. We describe the limitations of WWW access to data, and go on to explain the importance of good data models in managing collections of data with examples from our own experience with protein structure data. Next, we discuss the difficulties of building and maintaining such datamodels as the science evolves. We then describe alternative architectures for integrating distributed heterogeneous data resources, arguing for adopting a federated multi-database approach. Finally, we examine the role of CORBA in database integration.

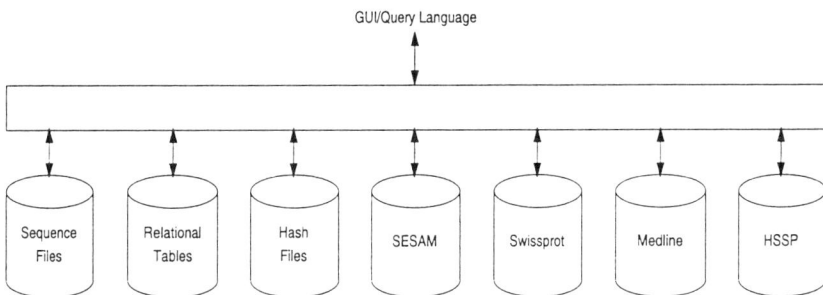

FIG. 3.1. Users should be able to access heterogeneous distributed bioinformatics resources via a single query language or graphical user interface.

CHARACTERISTICS OF BIOLOGICAL
AND NEUROLOGICAL DATA

Biological and neurological data resources share many of the characteristics found in scientific database in general. First, the pattern of updates is different to that in many commercial database applications (e.g., booking airline tickets where there is much cancellation and rebooking). Instead, as new observations are made, these are added to the database, and only if an observation is found to be incorrect will its entry be changed or removed. Therefore, the database tends to grow monotonically. As well as adding more instances of the same kind of data, new kinds of data items and named properties are introduced and new kinds of relationships between data items are added as these are identified to be of interest. Therefore, it is to be expected that the model used to describe the data will itself evolve as the database is used.

Data curation is a task performed by experts in the field, and their annotations contribute considerably to the value of a data resource. Further annotations will be added as the system is used, and may be a few words or several pages of description. In bioinformatics, an example of this is annotations in the Swissprot protein sequence databank. These include descriptions of the protein's function, and structural features of interest. In neuroinformatics, annotations enhance the information contained in images, such as magnetic resonance images showing lesions and other abnormalities.

There is a major role for annotations of cross-sectional 2D and reconstructed 3D models of the brain (Davidson & Baldock, 1997). These can be used to study the brain at various stages of development. There is some analogy with 2D earth satellite images and the corresponding reconstructed contour maps held in geographic information systems (GIS), but there is a closer connection with computer tomography that does reconstruction from Nuclear Magnetic Resonance signals. The significant feature again is the attachment of expert annotations to points and regions in the images, either just as labels or with comments. These annotations need to be held in a database that can be searched and queried using different techniques from those required to search the image data, but still retaining the ability to cross-reference between them.

In this connection, one should beware of storing data in proprietary representations used by web-based graphics or GIS packages, only to find out that this representation cannot be queried or used for other purposes. Many packages have their be-all and end-all in the graphical presentation of information, possibly interactive 3D displays, but we need to remember that what is informative to a human viewing a screen may not be at all accessible to remote automatic analysis programs. It is important that annotations are structured using a consistent vocabulary of terms, rather than free-form text, because this will enable efficient indexing and searching.

Bioinformatics and neuroinformatics must not be seen as disjoint fields. There are already areas of overlap and this will increase as our understanding of the molecular basis of brain function increases, and databases in both disciplines can benefit from links to medical literature databases. For example, mutations in particular genes can result in proteins that interact in some way, giving rise to degenerative brain disorders. The brain disorder CADASIL is an example of this, where mutations in EGF-like domains have been observed in patients with the disorder (Joutel et al., 1997). Correlating these mutations with structural data can suggest how the surface of these domains will differ in patients with the mutation, and how these domains may associate differently. Thus, in drawing together relevant information we want to be able to link databases from several areas (neurological images, protein structure, genetic sequences, and medical literature) because this may give us insights into the molecular and genetic basis of these disorders.

Another type of database is that giving relationships between genes in certain positions on chromosomes and the observable changes in development of eye or brain structures in flies as a result of gene mutations (see http://www.ebi.ac.uk/flybase & http://flybrain.uni-freiburg.de/). Here we have linkages (or relationships) between labelled images and genome sequences. We note that, in general, there is much greater use of image data in neuroinformatics, because many experimental observations are in this form, and are relatively easy to interpret. By contrast, in bioinformatics we are usually more interested in the summary interpretations of direct experiments. For example, the raw data on NMR spectra or reconstructed electron density are viewable as images, but we are generally more interested in information about molecular structure derived from these.

As a final and very challenging example of databases in neuroinformatics we consider the SenseLab project at Yale. This aims to integrate experimental data at different levels into a comprehensive model of an accessible neural system—the olfactory system. The initial work has resulted in a database of olfactory receptor sequences (http://crepe.med.yale.edu/ORDB/HTML/) and a database of neurons of the olfactory pathway (http://senselab.med.yale.edu/neurondb/), which are gradually being linked together. Here the receptor sequences are recorded in a form similar to bioinformatics databases such as GenBank, but with extra olfaction-specific data fields. However the neuronal data are complex and multidisciplinary, presenting challenging problems of data integration into functional models. The difficulty lies in finding a canonical framework that not only allows useful simulation and abstraction of neuron behavior but also allows accurate categorization of neuron structures to a level of detail that satisfies the anatomists! They are committed to a federated approach, so that they can link in related databases as the project evolves, and are experimenting with WWW interfaces to data in an Object-Relational database. This is a very similar philosophy to our own, as described later.

WWW TECHNOLOGY:
ITS USES AND SHORTCOMINGS

The World Wide Web has evolved to suit human users, who tend to search for particular pages of interest, controlling navigation interactively. It can also provide forms-based front ends for submission of data values or parameters to packaged queries. The answers may then be returned as lists of strings as in the case of genome or protein sequences, or even as stored images to be clicked through, possibly indexed by a menu of keywords.

More elaborate graphical presentations can be generated on demand by programs running on the server, which are invoked via the Common Gateway Interface (CGI). They could also be generated by Java programs (in the form of applets, which are certified not to have hidden side-effects when run on the client machine). The Java programs can interface to relational databases, by passing generated SQL queries through routines in the JDBC library, which spans many platforms. They can also connect to object databases or remote applications through cross-platform CORBA interfaces, as discussed in a later section. These are more advanced facilities, but here we discuss the basic use of web pages and HTML files to store data. This is tempting, because of ease of access by other researchers, but it has shortcomings as is seen here.

Approximate Search. The search techniques used are those evolved by the Information Retrieval community for free-format text. Because the program does not understand the text, it uses probabilistic matching, for example by scoring keywords, and expects to retrieve some false matches. Database queries, by contrast, are expected to return sets that exactly fit the given criteria, and may involve numerical comparisons. The data model they use effectively describes the meaning of data in the form of carefully checked formatted records, and does not have to deal with free-format natural language sentence structures. This is what allows queries to be more precise.

Lack of Type Check. The HTML format allows for some checks, but basically a URL embedded in a webpage can point to any other kind of page! You may be expecting an image, but get a table! Contents of databases, by contrast, are carefully type checked both on loading and updating. If a relationship is stored, linking to an object of another entity class, then that is what will be retrieved, not an object from some unexpected class. Further checks can be enforced, by expressing integrity constraints peculiar to a given class in a constraint language, and then storing them with the meta data that describes the database (Embury & Gray, 1995). For example, in our P/FDM database we can express the constraint that disulphide bonds in stored protein structures must be between cysteine residues in the following formal fashion:

```
constrain each r in residue such that
      some sc in sub_component has disulphide(sc) = r
to have name(r) = "cysteine";
```

Programs Can't Click. Web interfaces are designed to respond to mouse-click events, which trigger appropriate parametrised routines depending on screen location. However, a remote program cannot usefully emulate mouse-clicks. Instead, it is much more convenient to emulate a human typing to a command line interface because it only has to generate a text string according to a given syntax. Humans may be bored by command lines but computers love them! They are concise,easy to copy and send on to another machine, and their syntax can be carefully checked. CORBA interfaces are easily adapted to use them.

Set at a Time, Not Page at a Time Web interfaces are good at helping you to find a specific page, together with closely linked pages. They are not good at combining sets of similar objects taken from multiple pages, or at extracting sets of tuples of the same type. This is a routine job for a database query. Instead of following hypertext links, relational database systems use so-called foreign keys as tags to cross-reference tuples containing related data in other tables. These tuples can then be filtered and used to access other data. The results can be very large sets that need efficient processing. A bioinformatics example is the search for a set of fragments of protein backbone whose 3D folded shape is suitable for homology modelling of a new protein sequence. There can be many such fragments, and the search techniques needed to find them can be complex (Kemp, 1991).

Efficient Search. Some may argue that a set of indexed web pages constitutes a primitive database. However, the search capabilities provided are far below what one would expect from a database management system. When web pages are indexed for searching, this usually takes the form of a keyword index that enables searches for links to pages containing a specified word or phrase. Hypertext links between web pages do provide a kind of index for interactive browsing, but these links cannot be queried easily by automatic programs. If one does implement an automatic searching program that can follow links to retrieve related pages, then it is still necessary for the related pages to be retrieved one-at-a-time (see previous text) and for these to be processed on the client machine—each would have to be scanned sequentially to see if it matches the search criteria. It is more efficient to send selection conditions across to a remote part of a distributed database and to send back just the items required than it is to transport the data as whole web pages including images, only to reject much of it on arrival.

Despite the shortcomings of web pages for storing data per se, there is no doubt that web browsers are a good way to view the results of structured database searches, and that they are becoming a universal end-user interface. Thus, a better way forward is to hold the basic data in a structured database according to a data model, and to provide interfaces that generate web pages on demand in order to browse the data. It even may be possible to give the illusion of querying the generated pages for selected results, while the actual results are produced by generated database queries run on the underlying data. Some commercial web databases used for searching for flats and accommodation already use this technique.

MOTIVATION AND DEVELOPMENT
OF CONCEPTUAL DATA MODELS

An important first step in developing a computer-based data resource is to capture descriptions of objects in the real world, the relationships between them, and constraints on their relationships and properties. This process is known as *conceptual data modelling*. The result of conceptual data modelling is a formal description of our perception of the data we wish to store. We refer to this as our conceptual data model or schema. This allows a choice of ways to store the data. We call this separation of logical structure from physical realization the principal of *data independence*.

The most straight-forward way to store data within a computer is to use flat files. The Protein Data Bank (Bernstein et al., 1977) is an example of this. Data are simply stored as plain text files, which are formatted in some regular way. Application programs that use this data must read these files. Therefore, all programs must carry the overhead of having code for reading data from files. Flat files offer a "primitive" data model that cannot, for example,represent directly relationships among the data. Access to data in flat files is sequential, and application programs must scan through the files to find records of interest.

More flexible access can be achieved by using a database management system. Different database management systems provide different data handling and modelling capabilities, depending on the data model on which a system is based. The three classical data models are the relational model, the hierarchical model and the network model, and are described by Date (1977). In systems based on these classical models much effort is often needed to coerce the data into a suitable form for storage because the logical representation of the data was considerably different from the user's conceptual view of the application (e.g., none can support subclass relationships directly).

To address this difference, or semantic gap, an area of database research led to the development of semantic data models, in which the logical organization of data more closely resembles the conceptual model. Surveys of semantic data models have been carried out by Hull and King (1987) and Peckham and Maryanski (1988). Semantic data models represent entities and the relationships between them directly, and match closely our conceptual view of data. In our own work we use a very general and rich semantic data model called the *Functional Data Model* (FDM; Shipman, 1981).

Semantic data modelling uses abstraction mechanisms as tools for organizing data. The three main abstraction mechanisms are classification, aggregation, and generalization (Borgida, Mylopoulos, & Wong, 1984). These mechanisms are also present in modern object models.

> *Classification.* Entities that share common characteristics are grouped together as instances of a class. For example, if there are instances representing the individual proteins haemoglobin, gamma-chymotrypsin, and so forth, then these can be grouped together into the class molecular complex.
>
> *Aggregation.* This involves regarding a collection of values as properties of a single compound object or aggregate. For example, name, source and function can be considered as some of the constituent properties of a molecular complex object. Thus the class molecular complex is defined as an aggregation of its constituent properties.
>
> *Generalization.* If two or more classes have characteristics in common, then these commonalities can be abstracted into a general class. For example, the classes helix and strand will have many attributes in common (e.g., their associated chain, and length in residues). Thus, a more general class can be introduced to emphasize these similarities, and both helix and strand will be subclasses, or specializations, of this more general class. Attributes particular to either subclass will be represented by the appropriate subclass, (e.g. strands will be related to a beta-sheet but helices will not, so a relationship to represent this will be declared on the class strand, rather than on the superclass).

Representing the conceptual data model using a semantic model (such as the Functional Data Model) has several useful features for data integration.

> *Named Framework for Persistent Data.* A conceptual data model includes a description of the data to be stored in the database. This in-

volves identifying and naming objects, attributes and relationships that are to be stored, thus we identify what data are to be persistent compared to evanescent data that are used only within application programs. The names selected provide a common vocabulary for referring to data items.

Semantic Checks. Constraints on attributes and relationships are also recorded in the conceptual data model, providing semantic checks that can be incorporated into data verification programs.

Keys. For each object class proposed, a set of attributes and relationships are selected whose values will be unique for each instance of the class. Together, these selected properties form a key for a class. Keys make loading and exchanging data possible, enabling other data values to be associated with the right object instance. To store any data values about an object, it is necessary that at least the data values forming the key of that object must be stored (Paton & Gray, 1988).

Easily Extended. The conceptual data model is designed to accommodate future extensions as new sources of data become available. It provides a framework to which new classes and relationships can be added, as well as allowing new attributes to be added to existing classes (see later section on evolution of the model).

Data Independence

Scientific data are shared by many users who may want to use the data in different ways, including ways that cannot be predicted by the system designer. Their varied requirements mean that it is necessary to provide flexible access to the data. Central to achieving this is the principal of data independence (Gray & Kemp, 1994). Data independence originally came out of the ANSI-SPARC three-layer model (Ansi, 1975). It demanded that database systems be constructed so that they provided both logical and physical data independence. Logical data independence provides that the conceptual data model (or *schema*) must be able to evolve without changing external application programs. Only view definitions and mappings may need changing, for example to replace access to a stored field by access to a derived field calculated from others in the revised schema. One should also be able to change constraints in the conceptual data model without needing to recompile the external schemas (Elmasri & Navathe, 1994). Physical data independence provides something different. It allows one to substitute a different physical storage schema for an existing one, and to reload the data into the new form of storage, without any change either to the conceptual data model or application programs. In general, this is done in order to change access paths or to install new indexes or to recluster information in order to overcome performance degradation as the database evolves. Much of this is done in modern relational systems, and some of it can be done without dumping and reloading the data, which is obviously an undesirable process.

The Challenge of a Shared Data Model

The challenge of a shared data model (or object model) is considerable. In commercial data processing systems the model is presented as an Entity-Relationship (ER) diagram, as in Fig. 3.2. It is highly abstract in that it represents the names of entity classes and subclasses (in boxes or ovals), and of relationships between them (using thin lines), but it does not represent individual entity instances. Thus, a box may be labelled to represent the whole class protein but not an instance such as ovalbumin. It also shows the cardinality of relationships—how few or how many entity instances can be related by the relationship to a given instance. This is shown by blobs or crows feet at each end of the relationship line, and it makes clear whether the relationship is optional or mandatory, one-to-one or one-to-many.

This graphical technique has now been adapted to object-oriented systems as the UML methodology (Fowler & Scott, 1997), using the OM/T notation of Rumbaugh (Rumbaugh, Blaha, & Premerlani, 1991). In object-oriented programming the diagrams are called object models. They have been adapted to show the methods (parametrised procedures) that are permitted to operate on the entities. They also show specialized subclasses (either joined by a thick line or as boxes within the superclass box) that can inherit behavior defined by methods on the superclass. Unfortunately, beginners tend to overuse subclasses instead of using them in combination of relationships. This is not surprising as there is still much to be understood about this process (Fowler & Scott, 1997; Gamma, Helm, Johnson, & Vlissides, 1994).

The effort and experience needed to make a data model or object model that will stand the test of time is considerable. Recently there has been a substantial project at the European Bioinformatics Institute (EBI) to make an object model in re-usable sections for various kinds of genome sequence database, including the procedures that will work on the stored objects. This can be inspected at http://corba.ebi.ac.uk/EMBL/embl.html. The aim is to make it much easier to compose programs from these procedures by a kind of visual programming that can work on objects retrieved from the databases (e.g., see http://industry.ebi.ac.uk/applab/). Thus, the diagram shows what are the legal connections between program components along which data objects can flow.

Figure 3.2 shows a shared data model for protein structures developed as part of the EU-funded BRIDGE project (Gray et al., 1996). It looks deceptively simple as a finished article, but in fact it evolved through many versions and much debate. Such debates are likely to recur for the following reasons:

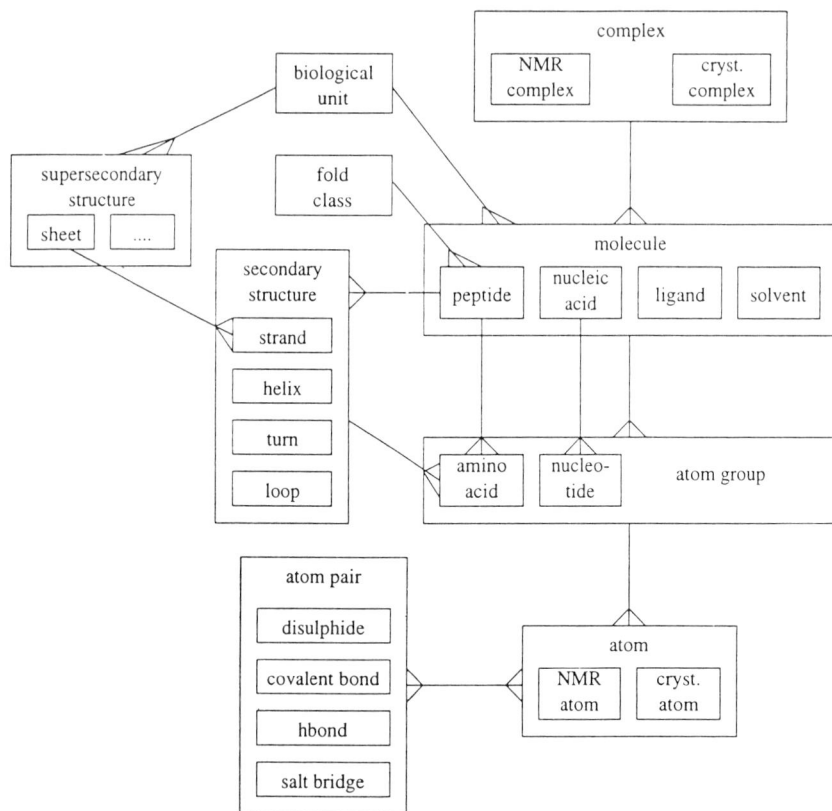

FIG. 3.2. Database schema for macromolecular structure. Each rectangle represents a class with certain properties or attributes. Relationships between classes are indicated by connecting lines. Some lines have *crow's feet* at the end, indicating a multi-valued relationship. A class can be specialized into subclasses that are like the parent superclass, but have extra attributes or relationships that only apply to the subclass. For example, *strand* is a subclass of *secondary structure* that is related to a *sheet*. It is shown as a rectangle within that for its superclass.

- People are too used to the way of naming or listing information in their own local database, and can't conceive of another more general way of doing it that adapts easily to suit other sites.

- Programmers have difficulty working at the abstract level of an ER model and tend to think in terms of familiar storage structures such as arrays or lists instead of recognizing them as different ways to represent a one-to-many relationship.

- Object-oriented programmers are so keen to re-use the behavior defined in some methods that they make otherwise unrelated entity classes into subclasses of a shared superclass despite a lack of biological or structural raison d'etre.

- Some items can be easily computed from other items, and vice-versa, so it is not clear which should be stored and which should be computed. If the computing takes a long time, then maybe both should be stored.

There can also be genuine scientific debate, especially where knowledge of the entities being modelled is evolving. For example, different interpretations of protein secondary structure elements are possible. The term secondary structure is used to describe backbone conformations within protein chains, and one example is the conformation called alpha helix. Although this term is commonly understood by those dealing with protein structures, there may be differences in the definitions used by different scientists, and these can result in differences of opinion regarding the locations of the endpoints of these structures. Indeed, two slightly different definitions are given by the nomenclature commission (IUPAC-IUB Commission, 1970), based on the presence of hydrogen bonding patterns. An operational definition has been implemented in programs that compute hydrogen bonds and secondary structure elements, (e.g., Kabsch & Sander, 1983), however, changing the parameters of these programs can result in different sets of hydrogen bonds being found and, hence, differences in the endpoints of secondary structure elements. Other differences can occur when a helix is kinked—should this be viewed as two short helices or one long kinked one? Another type of secondary structure element, strands, can also be viewed differently by different scientists. For example, some strands may contain a bulge in the middle that disrupts an otherwise regular hydrogen bonding pattern. Should the result be viewed as two short strands, or one long strand with a bulge? The argument becomes even more difficult where the corresponding protein in a related species does have a single long strand pair with uninterrupted bonding.

This is where we have to distinguish between storage of the data and storage of an interpretation of the data The helices and strands are a useful widely shared interpretation, but they are really in the eye of the beholder!It may even be necessary to store alternative interpretations according to another theory! What one wants to avoid doing is generating a combinatorial explosion of interpretations according to varying assumptions! In this case it is better to wait until theory has advanced and the interpretation is better understood before attempting to store it. If it is decided to store an interpretation, then that decision should be documented and data users should be in no doubt about any assumptions made in the stored interpretation.

Evolution of the Model

Even when a model has been designed it is essential that the version of it can evolve, with matching updates to stored data where needed to store rearranged information or extra information. This was recognized early on in database research and it was understood that the conceptual schema that formally describes the data model could evolve, but that exported views could be used to hide this, where needed, for example to give a consistent interface to legacy application programs. It was also understood that the underlying storage representation (which is chosen to give efficient access or update performance or some compromise)might well change without changing the data model. This is allowed by the principle of data independence. However, some users with home-made database systems break this principle in a shortsighted search for extra performance. They then find they have a totally inflexible data model tied to one particular storage representation, with a suite of programs that gets impossible to maintain! History shows that this should be avoided at all costs! It is one reason why good relational databases, which understood this, have lasted so well.

The easiest changes to make in an evolving model are those involving the addition of an extra named attribute to an existing entity class, or the introduction of a new entity class together with its properties (attributes). One can also introduce new relationships between existing entity classes. This commonly happens as science progresses and for example a new kind of experiment is introduced with measurements that need to be related back to existing entities such as proteins or brain regions.

It is also possible to replace a stored attribute by a rule or procedure that computes it from some more primitive properties. This can happen when observations which were thought to be independent turn out not to be.

Another useful mechanism is to introduce a new subclass that is a specialization of an existing class. An example of this in our protein schema is strand, which is a specialization of secondary structure. The instances of the subclass (technically a subtype) will have all the attributes of the existing entity class, and be counted as identifiable members of it, but they will also have extra attributes or relationships that are only meaningful for that subclass. This could be very useful for example,in distinguishing different regions of the brain, which behave uniformly with others in considering their geometric properties, but that have specialized biological properties. However, one must use subtyping in moderation; inexperienced modelers can easily create an explosion of combinations of subtypes!

These techniques, if used properly, can allow a model to evolve as scientific understanding advances, while continuing to make use of earlier experimental data, albeit at the cost of empty data values for some attributes. However, it requires constant watchfulness from experienced users, and expert advice from database modelers, or else it can slowly descend into a rats' nest! It is a similar problem to that involved in choosing additions to a programming language such as Fortran, where it becomes increasingly hard to retain compatibility with programs written for earlier versions. Fortunately, it is something we have learned to live with, and if we can cope with this kind of evolution, surely we can cope with data model evolution?

DATABASE INTEGRATION

As time goes on more types of databases will appear. The challenge is to integrate them in a flexible way that allows their continued expansion with local autonomy in updating, yet also allows us to automate search for answers to queries over the whole collection of databases. Two possible architectures for integrating biological database are described here in outline: a data replication approach and a federated approach (Sheth & Larson, 1990).

Data Replication Approach

In this architecture, all data from the various databases and databanks of interest would be copied to a single local data repository, under a single database management system. This approach is taken by Rieche and Dittrich (1994) who proposed an architecture in which the contents of biological databanks including the EMBL nucleotide sequence databank and Swissprot are imported into a central repository.

However, we believe that a data replication approach is not appropriate for this application domain for several reasons, which are as follows:

Space. The amount of biological data in existing databanks and databases is very large, and new data are being generated at an increasing rate. Few sites have sufficient disc space to mirror all data that may be needed by that site's users. Currently, national bioinformatics nodes provide a repository service for many databanks. However, a site wishing to integrate its private local data with the existing shared resources would be forced to mirror (at least part of) these.

Updates. Scientists want access to the most recent data. They want online access to results reported in the current journals as soon as these have been deposited in a databank or database. Whenever one of the contributing databases is updated the same update would have to be made to the data repository. (Changes and deletions are sometimes made to biological databases, but are much less frequent than additions.) Another possibility is for the data to be updated locally and periodically copied across to a central form, but then there is a delay in getting up to date information.

Autonomy. Significantly, by adopting a data repository approach the advantages of the individual heterogeneous systems are lost. For example, many biological data resources have their own customized graphical interfaces and search engines that will be tailored to the particular physical representation used with that data set. They also have their own update routines as noted later. The sociological importance of a measure of site autonomy must not be underestimated. People like to feel that they have control over their own data, and that they do not lose this when they start sharing data.

In summary, a data replication approach would require software, hardware, and human resources beyond what is reasonably available at each site wanting to use the data.

Federated Multi-Database Approach

We favor a federated approach that makes use of existing remote data sources, with data described in terms of entities, their attributes and relationships and their classes and subclasses. These are all described at a high-level in a shared data model, which is adaptable to a variety of physical storage formats used on participating databases.

Each of the databases exports a view of its tables or objects that conforms to the shared data model, so that queries can be expressed using a common set of names for properties and relationships regardless of the database. The queries are then translated so that they are actually run against the local data using local names in the local query language; in the reverse direction results may be scaled, if needed, to take account of a change of measurement units or character codes.

The technical challenge of these systems is to write programs with the intelligence required to split queries apart into subqueries to be translated and sent to local databases, and then to combine all the results that are returned. Great advances have been made in techniques for planning efficient distributed query execution and the component that does this is often called a mediator (Wiederhold, 1992).

With reference to the points previously listed:

Space. No extra space is needed locally, apart from a temporary cache for results retrieved from remote sites.

Updates. Because a single copy of the data is used with no local mirroring, all updates to the remote component databases are immediately available. The existing update programs can continue to run, using the local names and storage structures and indexes. If instead the data were to be copied into some centralized format on a centralized computer, there would be a great deal of work needed to rewrite the update programs.

Autonomy. A multi-database architecture does not affect other users of the component data resources who can, if they wish, continue to use these exactly as before. Furthermore, we can take advantage of customized software tools by sending requests to these from the mediator. One advantage of this is that the local query language can take advantage of indexing techniques that are locally available.

Thus there is no need to import large data sets from a variety of sources. Nor is it necessary to convert all data for use with a single physical storage schema. However, extra effort is needed to achieve a mapping from the component databases onto the conceptual model. The suitability of a federated multi-database approach for integrating biological databases is advocated by Robbins (1995) and also proposed by Karp (1995).

An Example Multi-Database System

In our current work, we are using the P/FDM database management system (Gray, Kulkarni, & Paton, 1992), which is based on a powerful shared Functional Data Model (FDM; Shipman, 1981), to provide access to data held in different physical formats and at different sites. The FDM and its query language, Daplex (similar to OQL), arose from the MULTIBASE project (Landers & Rosenberg, 1982) which was an early project in integrating distributed heterogeneous database systems. Another feature of FDM is that both stored and derived data are accessed in a uniform way, through functions (hence the name functional data model). This flexibility allows us to derive data through calls to remote databases.

Our main use of this database has been to support three-dimensional structural analysis and protein modelling (Gray, Paton, Kemp, & Fothergill, 1990; Kemp, 1991), and we have extended our initial general protein structure database to enable specialized techniques to be developed for modelling antibodies (Kemp, Jiao, Gray, & Fothergill, 1994; Ritchie & Kemp, 1997). A strong semantic data model like the FDM provides data independence, and we have experimented with several alternative physical storage formats, including hash files and relational tables (Kemp, Iriarte, & Gray, 1994).

Because this model uses object identifiers it is also potentially useful for federated access to the newer object databases that use object storage techniques (Cattell, 1997) and with hybrid Object-Relational databases. These latter have the advantage of storing many special data types such as images and sound, possibly in huge volumes, which can be cross referenced from the usual relational tables of numerical and character data (Brown & Stonebraker, 1995).

Our prototype federated system (Kemp, Dupont, & Gray, 1996) accesses biological databanks held at the European Bioinformatics Institute (EBI). These databanks consist of formatted flat files, and a system called the sequence retrieval system (SRS) maintains cross-references between related entries in different databanks held as indexes in separate tables. SRS also provides a command line interface that supports simple data selection requests. Our prototype system uses a description of the EBI databanks that maps these onto entities, relationships and attributes in an FDM schema. Queries submitted by the user are analyzed and partitioned automatically into parts that refer to data held locally and to data held at the EBI. Code generators construct data access requests to retrieve those data values from the local databases, and SRS code is produced and sent to the EBI for execution. This process is illustrated in Fig. 3.3 and Fig. 3.4 shows in detail the steps in processing a query that relates structural data in a local antibody database and data held at the EBI. Our P/FDM system is mainly implemented in the logic language Prolog, and query analysis and code generation is performed easily using Prolog's powerful pattern matching capabilities. The details of this are, of course, hidden from the end user, who uses the Daplex language or a graphical interface that generates it automatically.

Tight and Loose Coupling

Early Computing Science research concentrated on distributed database systems that were tightly coupled together and accessible through an integrated data model known as a global schema. This meant that the integrated model was designed before designing the schemas of the individual databases, which were dependent on it. This was done partly for performance and partly in order to guarantee consistency of global updates of pieces of linked data. Thus this model has tended to be used within large companies such as banks, but not across autonomous sites. The implementation made the shared data model very inflexible, so that when local databases had to evolve and add extra tables in different representations there was nowhere for this to be held in the shared model, and thus the extra information was not shared. Indeed, some observers became very pessimistic about global schema integration, and rejected it as impractical and requiring too much strong central management (Chorafas & Steinmann, 1993).

These pessimistic views began to change with the enormous success of the World Wide Web, which has shown that loosely coupled systems with only lo-

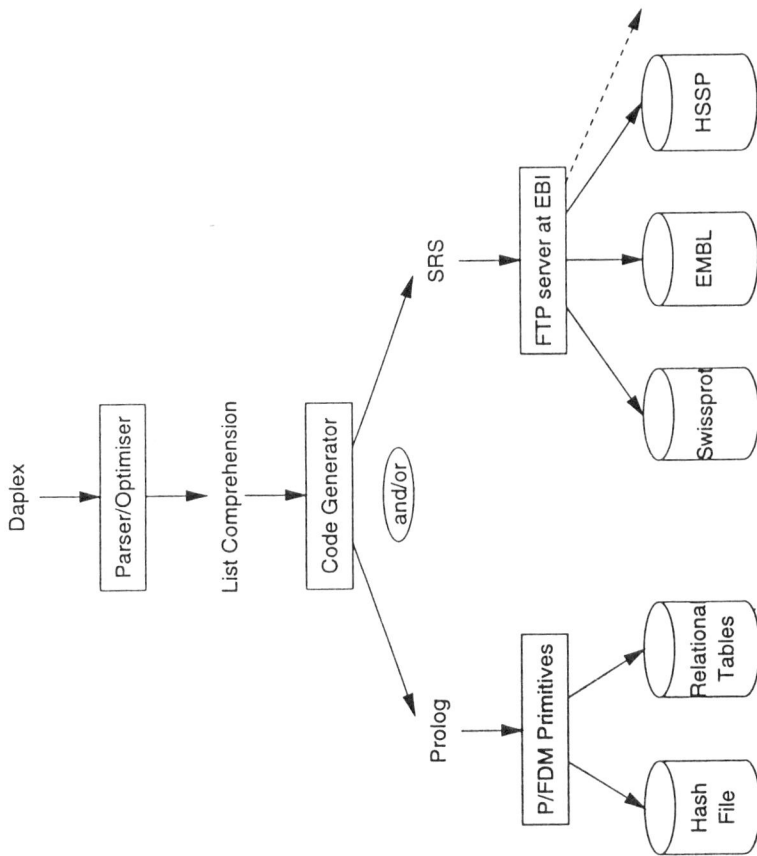

FIG. 3.3. A Daplex query may be translated into a Prolog query to access data held locally or SRS code to access data at EBI. However, some Daplex queries will need to access both local and remote data and so will be translated into a combination of Prolog and SRS code.

```
for each d in ig_domain such that name(d) = "VH"
    for each r1 in kabat_residue(d, "34")
        for each r2 in kabat_residue(d, "78") such that
            distance(atom(r1,"CB"), atom(r2,"CB")) < 5.0
            for each p in pdb_entry such that
                id(p) = protein_code(d)
                for each m in medline_entry such that
                    some l in link(p) has id(m) = l
print(protein_code(d), name(r1), name(r2),
    title(m), ref(m));
```

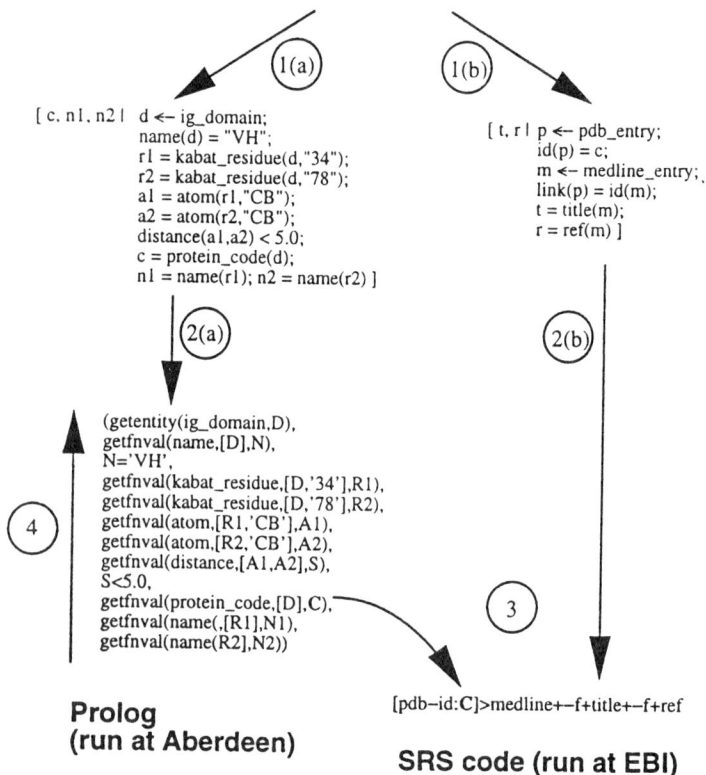

1(a)   1(b)

```
[ c, n1, n2 |  d ← ig_domain;
              name(d) = "VH";
              r1 = kabat_residue(d,"34");
              r2 = kabat_residue(d,"78");
              a1 = atom(r1,"CB");
              a2 = atom(r2,"CB");
              distance(a1,a2) < 5.0;
              c = protein_code(d);
              n1 = name(r1); n2 = name(r2) ]
```

```
[ t, r |  p ← pdb_entry;
          id(p) = c;
          m ← medline_entry;
          link(p) = id(m);
          t = title(m);
          r = ref(m) ]
```

2(a)   2(b)

4

```
(getentity(ig_domain,D),
getfnval(name,[D],N),
N='VH',
getfnval(kabat_residue,[D,'34'],R1),
getfnval(kabat_residue,[D,'78'],R2),
getfnval(atom,[R1,'CB'],A1),
getfnval(atom,[R2,'CB'],A2),
getfnval(distance,[A1,A2],S),
S<5.0,
getfnval(protein_code,[D],C),
getfnval(name,[R1],N1),
getfnval(name[R2],N2))
```

3

**Prolog
(run at Aberdeen)**

[pdb–id:C]>medline+–f+title+–f+ref

SRS code (run at EBI)

FIG. 3.4. An example query that accesses local and remote data. This query finds all heavy chain variable domains ("VH" domains) and examines the amino acid residues at positions "34" and "78" in the structural framework of the domain. The separation between their Cβ atoms is calculated and if this is less than 5.0 Angstroms a call is made to the FTP server at the EBI to find the titles and full references of all relate d articles. This query is processed as follows: 1. The Daplex query is translated to a list comprehension, which is split into two parts, (a) referring to local data and (b) remote data. 2. List comprehension (a) is translated to Prolog code including calls to the P/FDM primitive routines. List comprehension (b) is translated to SRS code. 3. The Prolog code is run at Aberdeen, providing a value for the variable C. For each value found, the value is added to the SRS code, which is then run at EBI. 4. Prolog backtracks to find other values for the variable C, and new SRS commands are sent to EBI.

cal updates can be remarkably flexible and effective. In this case users have been very willing to adjust their exported data to conform to a common syntax for marked up document (HTML) and a common protocol for exchanging messages (HTTP). The question is whether scientists with information to exchange will go one step further and use a shared data model, because the problem with WWW is that the information is now exchanged largely in natural language that computers can transport but not understand! Thus it is much harder for computers to process answers from autonomous web sites and be sure that the questions asked were interpreted consistently at each site!

The spectrum of choices for data integration is summarized in Fig. 3.5 (Robbins, 1995). At the top we have tight-coupling options that, as we have seen, are too restrictive. At the bottom we have an agreement solely on syntax, which corresponds roughly to the use of HTML. In order to get the desired federated information infrastructure we believe, with Robbins, that we do not require the adoption of a common hardware platform or vendor DBMS, but we do need a "shared datamodel across participating sites."

USING CORBA WITH SCIENTIFIC DATABASES

The Common Object Request Broker Architecture (CORBA) is an architecture standard proposed by the Object Management Group and widely supported by manufacturers. It provides a way to present an interface on the local machine to remote objects and their associated methods. CORBA is currently attracting widespread interest in the bioinformatics community as a technology that can assist in integrating distributed heterogeneous resources (e.g., the EMBL data model for genome data [http://corba.ebi.ac.uk/EMBL/embl.html]) is designed around the use of CORBA interfaces. We believe that CORBA can assist with the low-level integration of distributed software components and with wrap-

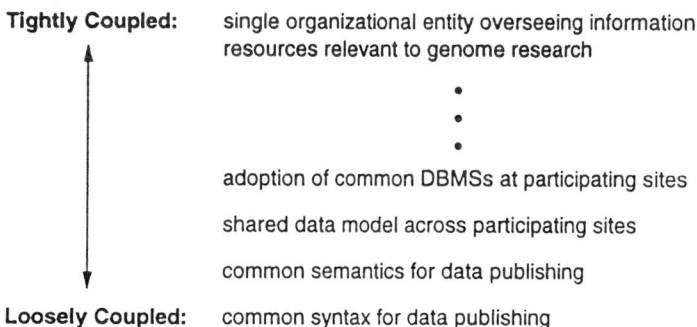

Tightly Coupled: single organizational entity overseeing information
                        resources relevant to genome research

                                    •
                                    •
                                    •

                        adoption of common DBMSs at participating sites

                        shared data model across participating sites

                        common semantics for data publishing

Loosely Coupled: common syntax for data publishing

FIG. 3.5. Continuum from tightly coupled to loosely coupled systems, involving multiple databases (from Robbins, 1995).

ping legacy systems. However, a straightforward mapping between CORBA objects and database objects can lead to inefficient systems and lose the benefits of data independence that database management systems, by definition, provide. In this section we describe the use and misuse of CORBA with database systems, and the difference between CORBA interface definitions and domain schemas.

Fine-Grained and Coarse-Grained Database Access with CORBA

Cormac McKenna (1996) described two alternative ways to use CORBA with an object-oriented database. That paper describes his experience using the ODB-II object database system and the DIAS CORBA-compliant ORB. In the first approach each OODB class and each OODB instance is represented as an ORB object. As an example, Fig. 3.6 shows how an interface to part of the conceptual data model shown in Fig. 3.2 can be defined in IDL. This approach requires the programmer to specify the execution plan in terms of the limited set of access functions provided in the IDL. Each step needed to achieve a task has to be programmed explicitly. This is laborious for the programmer and the resulting code is potentially very inefficient because an application task may require many small requests to be sent from the client to the database server and many small packets of data being sent from the client to the server (fine-grained access) with data selection being done on the client. McKenna commented that "the main difficulty with this approach is developing the infrastructure required to access objects from the database using queries" and that "queries cannot be passed very naturally to IDL methods."

In the second approach a single ORB object is used as the interface to the entire database, providing a server that can execute queries expressed in a high level query language. Here, the IDL resolves down to a single object rather than multiple objects that enables large queries containing several selections to be sent to the server for bulk execution (coarse-grained access), taking advantage of optimization strategies and indexes available on the server. McKenna's paper showed how queries expressed in ODQL (ODB-II's query language)can be embedded in C applications.

CORBA does not in itself provide a general purpose way to query data held at distributed sites. It supports distributed computing (use of behavior) but it doesn't help maintain and evolve distributed data. However, it does provide an architecture within which one can build the infrastructure and services to support the distribution of data. The language and platform independence that it promotes may give it an edge over sockets and remote procedure calls as a technology for enabling interprocess communication. As Object Request

```
module Protein {

        interface AtomGroup {
                integer                 position();
                string                  name();
                double                  phi();
                double                  psi();
        };

        interface Molecule {
                string                  molecule_id();
                integer                 num_residues();
                sequence<AtomGroup>     get_atom_groups();
        };

        interface Complex {
                string                  complex_code();
                string                  complex_name();
                string                  source();
                string                  authors();
                double                  resolution();
                sequence<Molecule>      get_molecules();
        };

        interface ProteinDatabase {
                sequence<Complex>       get_complexes()
        };

};
```

FIG. 3.6. Fine-grained COBRA IDL definition for an interface to part of the conceptual data model shown in Fig. 3.2.

Brokers become more freely available, we may see more client-server database applications migrating to CORBA. However, we believe that it is important that database services accessible through an Object Request Broker should at least allow coarse-grained access via a high level query language.

The relationship between CORBA and distributed databases is described by Brodie and Stonebraker (1995). They advocate that these should be viewed as complementary technologies, and that there are advantages in using software architectures that combine these. In section 8.1.5 of their book they suggested variants of a combined architecture, ranging from a "minimal database architecture" in which distributed DBMSs support just the data management functions declared in the IDL, to a "maximal database architecture" in which an entire distributed database solution is constructed and then a bridge is built to make this accessible from a CORBA environment. We believe that a "maximal database architecture" with a semantic data model at its heart is the best way forward when data integration, rather than distributed computation, is the main goal.

CORBA Does Not Itself Provide a Data Model

CORBA's interface definition language (IDL) is seen by some as an adequate way to represent data to be shared in a distributed environment. So why should anyone need a data model?

One needs to be aware of what objects are in the CORBA world. As seen in Fig. 3.6, to the onlooker IDL looks remarkably like a schema definition language used with an OODBS. However, more detailed examination shows that it plays a very different role. IDL is used to declare types that can be used in programs written in different languages and at different sites, and data values conforming to the IDL declarations can be passed between these programs. Rather than describing long term persistent data, it is better to think of IDL as a way of declaring structs of the kind seen in C, or equivalent type definitions in an OOPL. In doing this, CORBA IDL provides for language and platform independence but,significantly, it does not provide for data independence in the way that a data model does.

Thus, although CORBA IDL provides a good interface for programs, it provides nothing special for databases and must not be seen as a substitute for a proper data model.

CONCLUSIONS

We have looked at experience with building databases for shared community use in Bioinformatics, in search of lessons for the rapidly growing field of Neuroinformatics. The lesson from Computing Science research is to build databases according to the principle of Data Independence. This requires you to define a data model that gives a logical structure and names to various kinds of data, but that does not tie you to a particular storage structure. The actual storage may be anything from flat files to an object database, depending on considerations of performance and convenience.

Interestingly, CORBA interfaces also separate the exported public interface to a remote object from its implementation. However, as we have seen, this is more useful in making available remote procedures than in implementing a data model, because the notion of a high level query language independent of storage representation is lost. Nevertheless CORBA does provide valuable cross-platform working, and it can work well in implementing platform-independent gateways through which to send queries.

CORBA is also valuable in providing an interface through which remote programs may interact with data. This overcomes one of the main drawbacks of WWW interfaces, which is that they rely on mouse-clicks. The use of a datamodel also enables the remote program to understand about the data it is getting, whereas web pages rely too much on the natural language abilities of humans. Nevertheless, Web interfaces do provide a superb universally available and universally understood interface, and it is expected that databases will be accessed from the Web through a mixture of CGI scripts, Java applets, and automatically generated web pages that hide the kind of database software that is being used.

We have looked at the problems of integrating data from multiple databases and come down strongly in favor of a Federated system of loosely coupled databases accessed by mediator software. The databases need to export data conforming to a shared data model, in order that there be no confusion over the meaning of exported data values. However, this data model must also be able to evolve with time and we have reviewed our experience with this. We have also looked at a system constructed on these principles. Robbins put the challenge of evolution very succinctly: "Adding a new database to the federation should be no more difficult than adding another computer to the Internet." This challenge is harder than it sounds, because it requires people to understand the shared data model and to provide interfaces that export the right kind of data in the right form in response to queries against the shared data model.

Finally, we anticipate many new challenges in neuroinformatics. We have noted the prevalence of image data over coordinate data, and warned that annotations must be treated as data that may be queried and stored accordingly. People are investigating the challenge of storing data on neurons in some kind of canonical form. We look forward to the combination of data from bioinformatics and neuroinformatics in the search for understanding of complex biological systems.

ACKNOWLEDGMENTS

We are grateful for grants from the EU BRIDGE Programme and the BBSRC/EPSRC Joint Programme in Bioinformatics.

REFERENCES

ANSI (1975). Interim Report of the ANSI/X3/SPARC Study Group on Data Base Management Systems. *ACM SIGFIDET*, 7, 3–139.

Bernstein, F. C., Koetzle, T. F., Williams, G. J. B., Mayer, E. F., Bruce, M. D., Rodgers, J. R., Kennard, O., Shimanouchi, T., & Tasumi, M. (1977). The protein data bank: A computer-based archival file for macromolecular structures. *Journal of Molecular Biology, 112,* 535–542.

Borgida, A., Mylopoulos, J., & Wong, H. K. T. (1984). Generalization/specialization as a basis for software specification. In M. L. Brodie, J. Mylopoulos, & J. W. Schmidt (Eds.), *On conceptual modelling* (pp. 87–114). New York: Springer-Verlag.

Brodie, M. L., & Stonebraker, M. (1995). *Migrating legacy systems: Gateways, interfaces and the incremental approach.* San Francisco, CA: Morgan Kaufmann.

Brown, P., & Stonebraker, M. L. (1995). BigSur: A system for the management of earth science data. *Proceeding of the 21st International Conference on very large data bases VLDB'95,* pp. 720–728.

Cattell, R. G. G. (1997). *The object database standard: ODMG 2.0.* San Francisco, CA: Morgan Kaufmann.

Chen, I. A., & Markowitz, V. M. (1995). An overview of the object-protocol model (OPM) and OPM data management tools. *Information Systems, 20,* 393–418.

Chorafas, D. N., & Steinmann, H. (1993). *Solutions for networked databases.* New York: Academic Press.

Date, C. J. (1977). *An introduction to database systems* (2nd ed.). Reading, MA: Addison-Wesley.

Davidson, D., & Baldock, R. A. (1997). A 3-D atlas and gene-expression database of mouse development: Implications for a database of human development. In T. Strachan, S. Lindsay, & D. J. Wilson (Eds.), *Molecular genetics of early human development* (pp. 239–260). Oxford, England: BIOS Scientific Publishers.

Durbin, R., & Thierry-Mieg, J. (1992). *Syntactic definitions for the ACEDB data base manager.* [Online]. http://genome.cornell.edu/acedoc/syntax.html.

Elmasri, R., & Navathe, S. B. (1994). *Fundamentals of database systems* (2nd ed.). Redwood City, CA: Benjamin/Cummings.

Embury, S. M., & Gray, P. M. D. (1995). The declarative expression of semantic integrity in a database of protein structure. In A. Illaramendi & O. Diaz (Eds.), *Data management systems: Proceedings of the Basque International Workshop on Information Technology BIWIT 95* (pp. 216–224). Los Alamitos, CA: IEEE Computer Society Press.

Fowler, M., & Scott, K. (1997). *UML distilled.* Reading, MA: Addison-Wesley.

Gamma, E., Helm, R., Johnson, R., & Vlissides, J. (1994). *Design patterns.* Reading, MA: Addison-Wesley.

Gray, P. M. D., & Kemp, G. J. L. (1994). Object-oriented systems and data independence. In D. Patel, Y. Sun, & S. Patel (Eds.), *Proceedings of the International Conference on Object Oriented Information Systems* (pp. 3–24). Berlin: Springer-Verlag.

Gray, P. M. D., Kemp, G. J. L., Rawlings, C. J., Brown, N. P., Sander, C., Thornton, J. M., Orengo, C. M., Wodak, S. J., & Richelle, J. (1996). Macromolecular structure information and databases. *Trends in Biochemical Sciences, 21,* 251–256.

Gray, P. M. D., Kulkarni, K. G., & Paton, N. W. (1992). *Object-oriented databases: A semantic data model approach*. New York: Prentice Hall International Ltd.

Gray, P. M. D., Paton, N. W., Kemp, G. J. L., & Fothergill, J. E. (1990). An object-oriented database for protein structure analysis. *Protein Engineering, 3,* 235–243.

Hull, R., & King, R. (1987). Semantic database modeling: Survey, applications, and research issues. *ACM Computing Surveys, 19,* 201–260.

Huysmans, M., Richelle, J., & Wodak, S. J. (1991). SESAM: A relational database for structure and sequence of macromolecules. *Proteins: Structure, Function and Genetics, 11,* 59–76.

Islam, S. A., & Sternberg, M. J. E. (1989). A relational database of protein structures designed for flexible enquiries about conformation. *Protein Engineering, 2,* 431–442.

IUPAC-IUB Commission on Biochemical Nomenclature. (1970). Abbreviations and symbols for the description of the conformation of polypeptide chains. *European Journal of Biochemistry, 17,* 193–201.

Joutel, A., Vaheldi, K., Corpechot, C., Troesch, A., Chabriat, H., Vayssiere, C., Cruaud, C., Maciazek, J., Bousser, M.-G., Bach, J.-F., & Tournier-Lasserve, E. (1997). Strong clustering and stereotyped nature of Notch3 mutations in CADASIL patients. *The Lancet, 350,* 1511–1515.

Kabsch, W., & Sander, C. (1983). Dictionary of protein secondary structure: Pattern recognition of hydrogen-bonded and geometrical features. *Biopolymers, 22,* 2577–2637.

Karp, P. D. (1995). A vision of DB interoperation. *Meeting on the Interconnection of Molecular Biology Databases*. [Online], ftp://ftp.ai.sri.com/pub/oapers/karp-codata95.ps.Z.

Kemp, J. L. (1991). Protein modelling: A design application of an object-oriented database. In J. Gero (Ed.), *Proceedings of 1st international conference on artificial intelligence in design* (pp. 387–406). Oxford: Butterworth-Heinemann.

Kemp, G. J. L., Dupont, J., & Gray, P. M. D. (1996). Using the functional data model to integrate distributed biological data sources. In P. Svensson & J. C. French (Eds.), *Proceedings of the eighth international conference on scientific and statistical database management* (pp. 176–185). Los Alamitos, CA: IEEE Computer Society Press.

Kemp, G. J. L., Iriarte, J. J., & Gray, P. M. D. (1994). Efficient access to FDM objects stored in a relational database. In D. S. Bowers (Ed.), *Directions in databases: Proceedings of the Twelfth British National Conference on Databases* (BNCOD 12, pp. 170–186). Berlin: Springer-Verlag.

Kemp, G. J. L., Jiao, Z., Gray, P. M. D., & Fothergill, J. E. (1994). Combining computation with database access in biomolecular computing. In W. Litwin & T. Risch (Eds.), *Applications of databases: Proceedings of the first international conference* (pp. 317–335). Berlin: Springer-Verlag.

Landers, T., & Rosenberg, R. L. (1982). An overview of MULTIBASE. In H.-J. Schneider (Ed.), *Distributed data bases*. Amsterdam: North-Holland.

McKenna, C. (1996, May). Integrating the Object Database System, ODB-II with Object Request Brokers. *ICL Technical Journal,* 1–13.

Paton, N. W., & Gray, P. M. D. (1988). Identification of database objects by key. In K. Dittrich (Ed.), *Advances in object-oriented databases (Proceedings of Object-Oriented Database System-II)* (pp. 280–285). Berlin: Springer-Verlag.

Peckham, J., & Maryanski, F. (1988). Semantic data models. *ACM Computing Surveys, 20*, 153–189.

Rieche, B., & Dittrich, K. R. (1994). A federated DBMS-based integrated environment for molecular biology. *Proceedings of the Seventh International Conference on Scientific and Statistical Database Management* (pp. 118–127). Berlin: Springer-Verlag.

Ritchie, D. W., & Kemp, G. J. L. (1997). Modeling antibody side chain conformations using heuristic database search. In T. Gaasterland, P. Karp, K. Karplus, C. Ouzounis, C. Sander, & A. Valencia (Eds.), *Proceedings of the Fifth International Conference on Intelligent Systems for Molecular Biology* (pp. 237–240). Menlo Park, NJ: AAAI Press.

Robbins, R. J. (1995). *BioInformatics: Essential infrastructure for global biology* [Online]. http://www.esp.org/oecd.pdf.

Rumbaugh, J., Blaha, M., & Premerlani, W. (1991). *Object-oriented modelling and design*. Englewood Cliffs, NJ: Prentice Hall.

Sheth, A. P., & Larson, J. A. (1990). Federated database systems for managing distributed, heterogeneous and autonomous databases. *ACM Computing Surveys, 22*, 183–236.

Shipman, D. W. (1981). The functional data model and the data language DAPLEX. *ACM Transactions on Database Systems, 6*(1), 140–173.

Wiederhold, G. (1992). Mediators in the architecture of future information systems. *IEEE Computer, 25*(3), 38–49.

4 ⋯ Electronic Collaboration in Molecular Biology

Graham Cameron
Patricia Rodriguez-Tomé
Rolf Apweiler
European Bioinformatics Institute

Throughout society the increasing sophistication of electronic mechanisms to store, manipulate and communicate information has transformed the way we work. In particular, the opportunities and pitfalls for science opened up by information technology are profound. Nowhere has this been more apparent than in molecular biology. The information of life—DNA coding for complex proteins involved in intricate biological processes—has become accessible during the last three decades of the 20th century; fortuitously an era when computer hardware and methodology has seen a comparable revolution.

The way scientists deal with data has been completely transformed. It is possible to collect, analyze, communicate and share huge amounts of information rapidly and accurately. The benefits are fantastic. Electronic communication enables a kind of collaboration hitherto unthinkable—even simple e-mail allows the collaborative authoring of documents by authors on opposite sides of the world in real time.

Molecular biology, driven by the need to deal with large volumes of information, was quick to embrace the electronic medium; particularly to build large collections of shared scientific information. Substantial international efforts now support databases of DNA sequences (Benson, Boguski, Lipman, Ostell, & Oullette, 1998; Stoesser et al., 1998; Tateno, Fukami-Kobayashi,

Hiyazaki, Sugawara, & Gojobori, 1998), protein sequences (Bairoch & Apweiler, 1998) and protein structures (Sussman et al., 1998). Genetic mapping information was captured in the Genome Database (Letovsky, Cottingham, Porter, & Li, 1998), which evolved into an important resource in the early stages of the Human Genome Project.

Aside from these major projects, numerous other shared information repositories developed:

- What had been paper publications took advantage of the electronic medium (e.g.,
  -FlyBase (1998) is the database incarnation of what had been the "Red Book" (Morgan, Bridges, & Sturtevant, 1925). This was begun by Bridges in 1925 and became the bible of *Drosophila* genetics, appearing in its last paper edition in 1992 (Lindsley & Zimm, 1992).
  -The definitive documentation of genetic disorders *Mendelian Inheritance in Man* (MIM), by Victor McKusick (1966) which first appeared in 1966 developed into the database system online MIM (OMIM) (http://www.nebi.nlm.nih.gov/omim/).

- Personal files of research interest evolved into databases (e.g.,
  -Transfac (Heinemeyer et al., 1999) began its life as a collection of information about transcription factors generated out of the enthusiasm of a few researchers).
  -The P53 database (Hainaut et al., 1998) documents crucial information in the P53 gene, often implicated in cancer. It is one of a few hundred such databases concentrating on variations in individual genes of medical significance.

- Specialist subject areas developed their own databases (e.g.,
  -IMGT (Lefranc et al., 1999) the immunogenetics database, gives detailed information on genes relevant to the immune system).
  -ACEdb (http://www.sanger.ac.uk/software/Acedbl) is a comprehensive collection of information about a key model organism, the nematode *Caenorhabditis elegans*.

In the late 20th century, access to and skill in exploiting electronic information repositories is crucial to biological research. This sharing of information is typical of electronic collaboration in molecular biology, and it is on such shared repositories that this chapter concentrates. Other exploitations of electronic methods by collaborating molecular biologists, such as the use of e-mail, World-Wide-Web publication, and newsgroups all are immensely valuable, but biology is unlikely to yield insight that cannot be gained from other disciplines.

The January 1999 issue of the journal *Nucleic Acids Research* contains articles on some 90 databases, and this is just a small fraction of the collections available. The SRS server at the European Bioinformatics Institute (http://srs.ebi.ac.uk/) lists 362 different data banks (March 1999).

Unfortunately, these databases are not without their problems. Exploiting the complexity of the biological information using sophisticated information technology requires substantial technical expertise, and the volume of information is growing exponentially. Often important information resources have grown out of the personal files of biologists who never conceived of themselves as database designers. As a result, although there is a vast amount of valuable information, it often exists as islands, with little interconnection. It can be ill-defined and difficult to use, and there is little to help the user distinguish between high quality and low quality information.

It is nearly three decades since the establishment of the Protein Data Bank at Brookhaven National Laboratory in 1971, and already in 1980 the EMBL Nucleotide Sequence Database was established. Over the years such information resources have become invaluable to biological research, evidence that we got some things right, but many mistakes have been made and many lessons learned. With first-hand experience in the commission of historic database sins, we cast the rest of this chapter in the form of "Ten Commandments" of information sharing, with illustrations from molecular biology. They differ from the original 10 commandments in three respects (a) there are 12 of them, (b) they contradict each other, and (c) they represent the idiosyncratic and all-too-human views of the authors of this chapter.

We attempt to arrange these to give some kind of flow, but really what follows is a rather disjointed list. Although many of the issues are old-hat and well addressed in the language of computer science, we shy away from this approach, attempting to use common sense language. For those familiar with good database practice, we apologize for often stating the obvious. Indeed the term *database* is widely used in biology to refer to any shared collection of information, irrespective of its (dis)organisation, or of whether it actually utilizes real database technology. Here we do not fight against this sloppy usage or the rather pragmatic methods used in biological information provision, but rather attempt to give guidelines that merit consideration irrespective of the technical environment.

CAPTURE EXPENSIVE AND USEFUL DATA
FOR POSTERITY

It is no accident that the Protein Data Bank established at Brookhaven National Laboratory in 1971 was one of biology's first shared electronic information resources. The biological behavior of proteins is intimately linked to their function. Pathological mutations in essential proteins are often typically those where sequence changes disrupt the structure and hence the function. Medical intervention often uses compounds whose biochemical activity depends on how they bind to proteins. Understanding this binding process requires knowledge of the structure of the molecules involved. In short, structural information about biological macromolecules is incredibly valuable.

Unfortunately, the determination of the structures is a complex and expensive process. Initially x-ray-crystallography was the only approach, but persuading proteins to crystallize was a black art, and the path from protein to crystal to raw data to solved structure was fraught with difficulty. It was often a project of some years to determine a structure for a given protein. Therefore, although the data were extremely useful, they were expensive to determine. Thus the motivation to secure them in public databases was high.

By now there have been considerable advances in the determination of structure by crystallographic methods, and Nuclear Magnetic Resonance (NMR) allows structural information to be determined from molecules in solution. However, the determination of DNA sequences and thereby protein sequences is incomparably easier. Hence, in 1998 the public collection of structures contained only about 7,000 entries, compared with a DNA sequence database of over 2 million sequences. The protein sequence database (SWISS-PROT+TrEMBL) contains about 200,000 sequences (December 1998).

The structures are of immense value. Securing them was a high priority, and scientists responded wisely to that need with the early creation of a public repository for the information.

MAKE IT EASY TO CAPTURE ALL THE NECESSARY DATA WHEN THEY ARE AVAILABLE

Few scientists carry out their research with the primary goal of getting data into data banks. Structures of molecules are determined by those interested in the function of those molecules. DNA sequences are often determined as part of a research program that requires that information. Most scientists, however, recognize the utility of comprehensive public repositories of information and see it as a duty to include their information in such collections. But it is a chore.

The early wisdom of structural biologists in ensuring that structures determined at vast expense were captured for posterity sadly solved their problem incompletely. The structures deposited were the result of extensive computational work on the raw data from which they were derived. Typically structure factors and information about the computations have been lost forever. This was partly because historically it was not obvious how interpretative the process was—scientists deluded themselves into thinking that there was single correct interpretation of the data; and partly because the analysis and refinement took place over many months with much backtracking and reworking—often the original data and the details of the computation were not to hand when the structure was deposited.

Having seen the importance of capturing the structure information, we failed to capture all the necessary information when it was available. Hopefully new methods under development (Henrick, 1998) will rectify this.

BE PROACTIVE ABOUT ACQUIRING DATA

To get data from the scientific community you need to be proactive and prompt users to submit new data and to update existing data. It is necessary to make life for the submitters as easy as possible and to point them to the methods available to submit and update data. The publishers of most scientific journals now request that authors submit sequence and structure data to the databases. In their guidelines for authors they point the scientists to the DDBJ/EMBL/GenBank nucleotide sequence databases, SWISS-PROT and PDB. This did not happen overnight: It took some time to convince publishers to make submission of the sequence and structure data mandatory. The databases had to prove that they are proactive and make the submission procedure as easy as possible. They had to draft specific rules for authors so as to indicate what data authors need to submit to the relevant database(s) and what rules they should follow. And the submission mechanisms changed during the years. At the end of the 1980s, as the EMBL nucleotide sequence database pioneered the direct submission of sequence data, the EMBL database received most submissions on paper, in some cases with the sequences on discs. That shifted more and more toward submission by e-mail and now most of the data is submitted via the WWW. But even now the EMBL database offers a variety of mechanisms for submission and updating to allow the submitters to choose the method best suited to their special needs.

The Web-based sequence submission system 'Webin' (http://www.ebi.ac.uk/submission/webin.html) is EBI's preferred submission medium. Webin allows submission of sequence data and descriptive information by navigating the user through a series of WWW forms in an interactive and straightforward way. Database programmers and curators are continuously making improvements to Webin based on feedback from users and internal input, with the aim of further automation of the submission procedure. Submitters are also encouraged to report changes to the sequence, features, gene or product nomenclature and to send full citation information to the database when their sequence data are published (http://www.ebi.ac.uk/ebi_docs/update.html).

Another way to submit data is to use Sequin. Sequin is a multi-platform (Mac/PC/Unix) stand-alone software tool developed by the NCBI for submitting entries to the EMBL, GenBank, or DDBJ sequence databases (http://ftp.ebi.ac.uk/pub/software/sequin). To submit and update sequences via e-mail users can get a computer-readable data submission form from the EBI WWW-server (ftp://www.ebi.ac.uk/subs/allsubs.html), by electronic mail via the EBI fileserver (*netserv@ebi.ac.uk*), and with all releases of the EMBL Nucleotide Sequence Database. A computer-readable update form is available by e-mail (*update@ebi.ac.uk*) on request or by anonymous FTP (ftp://ftp.ebi.ac.uk/pub/databases/embl/release/update.doc).

Authors planning to submit a large number of similar sequences (i.e., > 25) on a single occasion are encouraged to contact the EMBL database before submitting the data. Database staff will then assist in making the submission of this specific data as convenient as possible, thus saving the author the time and effort required to complete numerous submission events individually.

Submissions from large sequencing projects are treated in a special way. The EMBL database has developed automatic procedures to allow the direct submission and incorporation of genome sequences such that new projects can be accommodated easily. Through all stages, EBI biologists communicate with the sequencing groups. A direct dataflow to the EMBL Database from various international sequencing efforts exists to ensure immediate incorporation and distribution of new sequence data and descriptive information. Particularly noteworthy is the collaboration on high-throughput data acquisition with the genome projects in the Sanger Centre, the most productive sequencing centre in the world.

SWISS-PROT and PDB also try to make the submission and update of protein sequence and structure data as easy as possible for the scientific community by offering a variety of ways to submit and update data (http://www.ebi.ac.uk/n.sp/submissions.html, http://autodep.ebi.ac.uk/autodep_basepase.shtml). SWISS-PROT has also built an extensive network of experts, which provide us with valuable information (http://www.exposy.cb/cyi-bin/experts). The SWISS-PROT group at the EBI has recently set up a prototype collaboration with the *Protein Profile* series published Oxford University Press. An issue of "Protein Profile" gives a comprehensive review about certain protein families. A SWISS-PROT curator creates a list of all SWISS-PROT and TrEMBL entries currently available for a particular protein family. This is sent to the authors by e-mail. The authors will revise, correct and add to the entries any annotation information they have available. The updated or new entries will be sent back by e-mail to the curator at the EBI. The curator will check and correct the updated or new entries and integrate the data into the SWISS-PROT database. The curator creates tables and alignments for the protein families and makes them online available (http://www.ebi.ac.uk/services/protein_profiles/). Oxford University Press links from their *Protein Profile* online version to the data in SWISS-PROT and to the tables and alignments at EBI.

Such an electronic collaboration is very beneficial for both sides, because we combine the biological expert knowledge of the authors with the EBI's expertise in data management, bioinformatics and sequence analysis.

But even if you make submission and updating as easy as possible, it will only get used when you make users aware of it. It is absolutely crucial to get the message to your potential submitters and you need to follow many different routes: advertisements, announcements in newsgroups, newsletters, database release notes, spreading the news in talks and posters at conferences, personal contacts, etc. Only through the participation of database curators in the education of the life science community can we come closer to the goal of getting all the valuable experimental data submitted to databases.

MAKE IT EASY TO GET AT THE MOST FREQUENTLY USED DATA

It's easy to let the ready availability of vast storage devices go to our head. We want to preserve all the information under the sun, often in the absence of any consideration of how the information will be used. One should distinguish between information that is stored because it may sometime be useful (an archive), and information that will be heavily used (a library).

Anyone who's used the World Wide Web will be well aware how hard it is to extract useful information from a forest of irrelevance.

In building the DNA sequence databases, we were acutely aware of the huge demand for a comprehensive, up-to-date collection of sequence data. The best way to achieve this was to follow our exhortations above, and capture the information direct from researchers. After some early negotiations, scientists and journal editors collaborated with us to ensure that data were directly deposited, and a scheme evolved that works well today, with a new sequence entering the database once a minute.

Of course data are seldom perfect, and sequence data are no exception. Sequences contain errors, and regions of low confidence. Depositors often would like to indicate which regions are dubious, and, in these days of automatic sequencing, some centers have expressed an interest in depositing the sequence traces—the raw data from which the base sequences are inferred. Seen from an experimentalist's point of view, this is attractive, but in truth it would be an unusual user of the sequence database who would use the information, and certainly current sequence analysis systems offer little help in manipulating such data.

Currently we do not include the traces in the general-purpose database, but typically sequencing centers archive such data so that they can be retrieved as necessary. This seems a sensible compromise—build a real library for the data in daily use, and an archive for the raw data, which may be useful.

DON'T COMPLICATE EVERYONE'S LIFE FOR THE SAKE OF A FEW ESOTERIC CASES

Computer systems have an uncanny way of getting too complicated. We are all familiar with overblown word-processors with a plethora of esoteric options that baffle even their regular users. Information resources in science can easily suffer the same problem. Indeed it can be worse. Since they are typically community resources, often supported through public funding, there is a well-meaning desire to involve the community in their design. This is fine. In fact it would be hard to design a resource that would serve a particular community well without carefully gathering their requirements. But this is not tantamount to letting the community design the system.

Experience with the EMBL/GenBank/DDBJ feature table design is interesting in this respect. In May 1986 a group of people from the international sequence database activities got together in an attempt to design a standard "feature table" for the databases. The feature table is the information within the database, which gives information about points and regions in sequences. An important function is to tabulate regions, which code for proteins, but it is also used to indicate signal regions, variants, and even regions of uncertainty in the sequence. It became clear in the design process that the committee-style design had a flaw—it imposed no restraint on the complexity. Anyone in the group could add their favorite item to the specification, but no one actually vetoed anything. We produced a design that was astoundingly rich, capable of representing all the biological features we could imagine and, the evidence for them and the niceties of any uncertainty in that evidence. It had a problem. Ninety-nine percent of users wanted to use the feature table to deduce the protein sequence from reliably determined coding regions. They had no interest in about 26 pages of the 30-page definition, and we had rendered what they saw as a simple task incredibly complex. A number of rounds of pruning produced workable definition, a further evolved form of which is still in use today (http://www.ebi.ac.uk/ebi_docs/embl_db/ft/feature_table.html). It remains impressively complex. One feels that some of the complexity could have been avoided. And this wasn't community design. This was a group of about eight enthusiasts.

Community design is well exemplified in the development of the macromolecular Crystallographic Information Format (mmCIF). These are a set of format specifications that were developed to represent the structure of macromolecules. They include the three-dimensional coordinates of atoms and information about the molecules described and the process by which the structure was determined. The "CIF dictionaries" evolved over more than 10 years in a series of open meetings. Community spirit necessitated that methods to represent even the most esoteric if information be included, creating a burgeoning complexity without careful architecture. To their credit several groups have made systems based on mmCIF function, but it has been an uphill struggle.

The information in the mmCIF definitions, or the early ramblings of our feature table definition of course are useful, but they should have been boiled down to tight specifications of the crucial concepts.

WORRY ABOUT TODAY'S DATA, WORRY MORE ABOUT TOMORROW'S—YESTERDAY'S WILL SOON BE HISTORY

For hundreds of years most scientific work has been published on paper, and only recently journals began to request the submission of certain information to databases. That means that everyone running a scientific database needs to consider how much time and effort should be spent on scanning the literature and contacting scientists for additional information. The SWISS-PROT protein sequence data bank, for example, strives to provide a high level of annotation (such as the description of the function of a protein, its domain structure, post-translational modifications, variants, etc.), a minimal level of redundancy and high level of integration with other databases. SWISS-PROT is not a protein sequence archive, but tries to provide a review of what is currently known about a given protein sequence. In doing so, our curators stumble across a lot of conflicts between the sequence data of different submitters claiming to have sequenced the same gene or the same protein. Very often even the same scientists contradict themselves, because the published sequence is different to the sequence submitted to the databases. The curators could spend most of their time sorting out these conflicts. And although it is of importance to mention conflicts in a SWISS-PROT entry and if possible to clarify the nature of the conflict (sequencing errors, typos, strain variations, polymorphism or revisions), we should always ask ourselves whether the sequence data is worth the effort. The amount of sequence data is doubling every year and our efforts may be much more rewarded when we try to capture the new data in a better way. Instead of spending too much time chasing errors in the historical data, we need to make sure that we get tomorrow's sequence data right.

LIBERATE THE INFORMATION

The limitations a database may face due to the ownership of parts of the data by individual submitters is another important issue. Traditionally, nucleotide sequence data, either of individual genes or of complete genomes, have been made publicly available by being deposited in the DDBJ/EMBL/GenBank nucleotide sequence databases. These data archives, which are a record of scientific achievement, are absolutely essential for research and exploitation. For several reasons, however, they cannot provide all of the resources that are needed by the scientific community. Scientifically, it is very important that these archives reflect the achievements of individual scientists. The scientific record can no more be changed by a third party than can the conventional scientific literature, published in journals or books, be rewritten by anyone other than its original authors. Just as the conventional scientific literature is redundant, so are the sequence archives; many genes will often be represented by many (sometimes thousands) of individual sequence records. The fate of many sequences is that researchers gain additional knowledge about them by subsequent research. This knowledge is reported, by and large, in the conventional literature and there is, nor can there be, any mechanism to integrate it with the original sequence. Finally, the constraints of the international agreement between the nucleotide sequence databases are such that some of the necessary changes in the data representation that are needed to evolve with the science are very hard to obtain.

To overcome these limitations the EBI works on a second generation of nucleotide sequence database. The relationship of this database (and of the SWISS-PROT protein sequence database) to the nucleotide sequence archives can be considered to be the same relationship that exists between a scholarly review of a field of scientific endeavor and the primary literature on which that review is based.

KNOW YOUR DOMAIN

It is also of importance to restrict yourself. If you design a scientific database work on a scientific problem in your domain, use the technology adequate to solve the problem, and store the data relevant for your domain. Do not try to reinvent the wheel. Use external authorities as much as possible. Instead of storing all sorts of data in your database build links to other specialized databases, collaborate by passing relevant information to them, and announce in advance changes (format, contents, or access methods) that may have an impact on other databases. In the release notes of every release of the EMBL nucleotide sequence database and of the SWISS-PROT protein sequence data bank you will find the announcements of planned changes to the databases. The reason is very simple: Science and technology changes and the databases need to make sure that they can evolve with the science. Design for change because you are bound to get it wrong. You can be sure that the redesign of your database will never end, and thus the adaptation of your database to scientific and technological advances will be less painful if you know your domain.

JUST BECAUSE A DATABASE IS ILL-DESIGNED, IT DOESN'T MEAN ITS CONTENTS AREN'T WORTH RESCUING

In the field of biomolecular databases many data resources have grown out of the personal data collections of biologists lacking the technical expertise for the full exploitation of the biological information. An example how database technology and enhanced interconnectivity can add value to the knowledge of the life scientists are the mutation databases. These databases typically arise out of clinical research needs. They are designed to meet the needs of a small group of researchers collecting information about mutations in one or few loci. This has lead to lack of coordination and standards in these databases making it difficult for other researches to access the data. Research groups have invested time and money into their databases and have understandably little interest in redoing them in other formats. To make these data resources more widely usable by the scientific community, the EBI started a project to find common data structures in various independent mutation databases and to create a unified access tool to query them individually and together (http://www2.ebi.ac.uk/mutations/central/srs_mutations.html). The interface is provided by the Sequence Retrieval System (SRS); (http://srs.ebi.ac.uk), which is a powerful tool for parsing, indexing, viewing and linking independent textual databases. Complex queries can be performed over multiple databases, custom views can be defined and the results of a query can be saved for further analysis. A collection of mutation database references has been made into a public database "List of Mutation Resources," MutRes (http://srs.ebi.ac.uk/srs5bin/gi_bin/wgetz?-fun+pagelibinfo+-info+MUTR ES). MutRes currently contains information on more than 170 mutation or related databases.

Not all these databases are available in their entirety for downloading across the Internet. Others have only limited access (e.g., for specific queries, or they are under construction). To date, starting from larger and more established databases, the EBI has made available through the SRS server 30 locus specific databases, together describing over 14,000 unique human mutations, a mitochondrial variation database, a gene mutagenesis database and four non-specific databases.

The nonspecific databases complement locus specific databases by larger coverage of different genes. Extraction of variation features from the DDBJ/EMBL/GenBank and SWISS-PROT sequence databases and OMIM into new secondary databases, EMBLCHANGE, SWISSCHANGE and OMIMALLELE, allows them to be searched and browsed together with the locus specific databases.

STANDARDIZE WHERE YOU NEED STANDARDS, DON'T WHERE YOU DON'T

To allow efficient querying of a database, it is necessary to store data consistently. In an ideal world every database would use the same completely controlled vocabulary, with exact definitions of the meaning of each and every term and with a precisely documented usage of every term in the database. In the real world this is impossible. The databases need to navigate between the demand for rapid incorporation of as much data as possible into the database and the demand for a controlled vocabulary. The rigorous usage of controlled vocabulary slows down the incorporation of new data into the database. Data-mining is a hopeless task without controlled vocabulary. The different biomolecular databases follow all different policies on controlled vocabulary. However, some standards should be followed by all life science databases. Of highest importance is to abide to the rules of the Joint Nomenclature Committee of IUPAC and the International Union of Biochemistry and Molecular Biology (JCBN IUPAC-IUBMB); (htp://www/chem/qmw.ac.uk/iupac/jcbn). The databases should also always use the Medline UID as identifiers for published journal citations and the Patent ID for patents citations.

The SWISS-PROT data bank is probably the database, which most rigorously enforces the specific rules of the relevant nomenclature committees concerning gene names, protein names, etc. SWISS-PROT publishes a constantly updated list of all available relevant nomenclature references (published or electronic) used by the protein sequence data bank (http://www/expasy.ch/cgi-bin/lists?nomlist.txt).

Because standardization and nomenclature are as much a user community task as a database task, and in order to prevent the further population of the databases with ambiguous vocabulary, we appeal to our users to consider the following before publishing or submitting to a database the name of a new protein or gene:

- Is such a name or acronym already in use in the international nucleotide sequence (EMBL/GenBank/DDBJ) and protein (SWISS-PROT) databases?
- Is such a gene name already in use in the relevant genomic database or genome nomenclature?
- Does such a gene name follow the specific guidelines for the specific organism from which it has been isolated?

- Have you performed a literature search using Medline or an equivalent database to check that the new proposed name does not clash with existing names?

- If there are compelling reasons to assign to a new biomolecular entity a name previously attributed to another biomolecular object, we strongly suggest that the publication or submission of the reassigned name be accompanied by a short explanation of why it was necessary to do so and in which context the name has already been used.

- One should not use the molecular weight of a protein as part of a gene name or a protein name. Molecular weights are generally not conserved across species and therefore their inclusion in any type of nomenclature will generate a significant amount of confusion.

IDENTIFIERS—KNOW THEIR SCOPE
AND PERSISTENCE

It is important to provide unique and stable identifiers to objects in a database that can be independently accessed. Unfortunately this is not as simple as it sounds. It is not a problem to attach to every object in a database a unique identifier, but how can you guarantee the stability of these identifiers during update cycles in the database? And how can you make users aware that a object in the database has been updated? In the following we use the synchronization of the coding sequence (CDS) features in the EMBL nucleotide sequence database with the SWISS-PROT + TrEMBL protein sequence database as an example to illustrate these problems.

In the past, the EMBL nucleotide sequence database and SWISS-PROT + TrEMBL cross-referenced each other on the level of entries, pointing to the unique identifier, the accession number, of the other database. Whenever an EMBL record changed, SWISS-PROT was informed that an update occurred, and a SWISS-PROT curator checked the corresponding SWISS-PROT entry and updated the record if necessary. Historically, most EMBL entries pointed to only one SWISS-PROT entry. However, with the start of the numerous genome projects, longer contiguous sequences were submitted, which contained numerous CDS. Each CDS pointed to a different SWISS-PROT + TrEMBL entry. If one CDS was updated, SWISS-PROT was informed that all proteins linked to this entry might be potentially in need of an update. Because one single EMBL entry can contain hundreds of CDS, it became impossible to find the affected SWISS-PROT entry among all the unaffected ones.

In this context, the need to linking at the CDS feature level is evident. This linking has now been achieved by using the Protein Identification number found in the protein_id qualifier tagged to every CDS in the EMBL nucleotide sequence database. The ProteinID consists of a stable ID portion plus a version extension. The version number will change only when the protein sequence coded by the CDS changes, while the stable part will remain unchanged. The DR (Database cross References) lines of SWISS-PROT and TrEMBL entries pointing to an EMBL database entry now cite the EMBL accession number as primary identifier and the ProteinID as secondary identifier.

In all cases where a ProteinID is already integrated into SWISS-PROT or TrEMBL a /db_xref qualifier citing the corresponding SWISS-PROT or TrEMBL entry is added to the EMBL nucleotide sequence database CDS labelled with this ProteinID. At regular intervals, a list of all SWISS-PROT and TrEMBL AC numbers and entry names together with the ProteinID numbers present in these SWISS-PROT and TrEMBL entries is passed to the EMBL nucleotide sequence database for cross-referencing purposes.

SWISS-PROT and TrEMBL receive in return at regular intervals the lists of ProteinID numbers no longer present in the EMBL database due to deletion of these ProteinID numbers, and of those with a changed version number. The SWISS-PROT and TrEMBL entries related to those ProteinID numbers are updated and the new full ProteinID list is given to EMBL for update of the /db_xref qualifiers in the next release.

This procedure allows a good synchronization between the two databases and enables us to point precisely from a given SWISS-PROT or TrEMBL entry to one of potentially many CDS in the corresponding EMBL entry and vice versa. This change allows software tools the automatic retrieval of that part of a nucleotide sequence entry that codes for a specific protein.

COSSET YOUR CURATORS

And now we discuss the final, but definitely one of the most important points. The quality of a database is highly dependent on the skills of its annotators. Databases should strive to attract top individuals as curators and put a lot of emphasis on further training. The SWISS-PROT database for instance would not be capable of providing such high quality information on proteins without the highly skilled and motivated life scientists doing the annotation. It is very important to train the annotators to be critical of any information whether published or not. SWISS-PROT encourages their curators to visit conferences and workshops to stay active in science, and to meet users and submitters. We also encourage our curators to visit other databases as a way to meet other annotators and to share their skills and experiences. The quality of a database always depends on the quality of the people entering the data!

REFERENCES

Bairoch, A., & Apweiler, R. (1998). The SWISS-PROT protein sequence data bank and its supplement TrEMBL in 1998. *Nucl. Acids Res.*, *26*, 38–42.

Benson, D. A., Boguski, M. S., Lipman, D. J., Ostell, J., & Oullette B. F. F. (1998). GenBank. *Nucl. Acids Res.*, *26*, 1–7.

FlyBase Consortium. (1998). Flybase: A *Drosophila* database. *Nucl. Acids Res.*, *26*, 85–88.

Hainaut, P., Hernandez, T., Robinson, A., Rodriguez-Tomé, P., Flores, T., Hollstein, M., Harris, C. C., & Montesano, R. (1998). IARC Database of p53 gene mutations in human tumors and cell lines: Updated compilation, revised formats and new visualization tools. *Nucl. Acids Res.*, *26*, 205–213.

Heinemeyer, T., Chen, X., Karas, H., Kel, A. E., Kel, O. V., Liebich, I., Meinhardt, T., Reuter, I., Schacherer, F., & Wingender, E. (1999) Expanding the TRANSFAC database towards an expert system of regulatory molecular mechanisms. *Nucl. Acids Res.*, *27*, 318–322.

Henrick, K. (1998). CCP4 and data harvesting. *CCP4 Newsletter on protein crystallography*, *35*, 13–16.

Lefranc, M. P., Giudicelli, V., Ginestoux, C., Bodmer, J., Mueller, W., Bontrop, R., Lemaitre, M., Malik, A. Barbie, V., & Chaume, D. (1999) IMGT, the international ImMunoGeneTics database. *Nucl. Acids Res.*, *27*, 209–212.

Letovsky, S. I., Cottingham, R. W., Porter, C. J., & Li, P. W. D. (1998). GDB: The human genome database. *Nucl. Acids Res.*, *26*, 94–99.

Lindsley, D. L., & Zimm, G. G. (1992). The genome of drosophila melanogaster. San Diego, CA: Academic Press.

McKusick, V. A. (1966). Mendelian inheritance in man: Catalogs of autosomal dominant, autosomal recessive, and X-linked phenotypes. Baltimore, MD: Johns Hopkins Press.

Morgan, T. H., Bridges, C. B., & Sturtevant, A. H. (1925). The genetics of Drosophila melanogaster. Bibliophis Genetics, *2*, 1–262.

Stoesser, G., Moseley, M. A., Sleep, J., McGowran, M., Garcia-Pastor, M., & Sterk, P. (1998). The EMBL nucleotide sequence database. *Nucl. Acids Res.*, *26*, 8–15.

Sussman, J. L., Lin, D., Jiang, J., Manning, N. O., Prilusky, J., Ritter, O., & Abola, E. E. (1998). Protein data bank (PDB): Database of three-dimensional structural information of biological macromolecules. *Acta Crystallographics, Section D (Biological Crystallography)*, *54*, 1078–1084.

Tateno, Y., Fukami-Kobayashi, K., Miyazaki, S., Sugawara, H., & Gojobori, T. (1998) DNA databank of Japan at work on genome sequence data. *Nucl. Acids Res.*, *26*, 16–20.

5

❖❖❖

Electronic Collaboration in Environmental and Physical Sciences Research

Richard T. Kouzes
West Virginia University

The Internet, crucial to the conduct of science, is now being used to create virtual collaborative laboratories, or *collaboratories*. A collaboratory is an open meta-laboratory spanning multiple geographical areas where collaborators interact via electronic means—"working together apart." Despite progress in technology that has allowed for successful network based scientific collaboration, many hurdles remain. In particular, the psychosocial barriers of human interaction over a limited electronic system inhibits the full success of collaboratory implementation. Application to the physical sciences and development of an environmental sciences collaboratory is discussed.

A COLLABORATORY SCENARIO

He along with his students had spent many lengthy days in his laboratory at Princeton University and in other places in his virtual laboratory space, doing all of the preparatory work. That morning he had met with his collaborators from around the country in an immersive teleconference to make the final plans for the experimental sequence that would answer some burning issues surrounding bioremediation of hazardous chemical waste. The experiment would begin shortly. He would be using the most advanced Nuclear Magnetic Resonance spectrometer available, a one giga-Hertz instrument located at the U.S. Department of Energy's Environmental Molecular Sciences Laboratory in Richland, Washington. He looked out of his window as the sun was setting over the Princeton Graduate College, then facing his computer, entered his virtual laboratory to begin collaborating with his colleagues a continent away. The sample they had prepared was in place in the 23 tesla magnet in Richland. Checking the settings for the NMR on his monitor, together they prepared to carry out the experiment. ...

THE COLLABORATORY VISION

The realization of a vision of telepresent scientific collaboration such as the scenario given above is limited today by two divergent yet interrelated factors. One is the state of today's technological capabilities, and the other is the psychosocial issues governing human interaction. In their book *Jumping the Curve*, Imparato and Harari (Imparato, 1994) spoke of processes and organizations moving forward through quantum jumps. We must make the quantum leap in technology and work methodology to realize solutions to the very complex issues faced today by science. Information technology now brings a method to expand and to democratize the membership of the scientific community. Most human activity consists of moving things from one place to another. Today, information is a commodity of great economic value, which can be transported globally via electronic means at a speed that doubles every 18 months.

Science has benefitted greatly from the computing revolution of the last four decades. However, although technology has made science as we know it possible, it has not yet impacted on the collaboration process itself to the degree we will see in the next 10 years. There is a future vision of computer enabled tele-present cooperative work that is far from the present state, yet we are beginning to take steps to reach our vision.

A *collaboratory* (a merger of the words "collaboration" and "laboratory") (Wulf, 1989) is an open meta-laboratory that spans multiple geographical areas with collaborators interacting via electronic means—"working together apart." Collaboratories are designed to enable close ties among scientists in a given research area, to promote collaborations involving scientists in diverse areas, to accelerate the development and dissemination of basic knowledge, and to minimize the time-lag between discovery and application. Creating a collaboratory entails integrating software and hardware computing tools to produce an environment where multiple, geographically separated researchers can collaborate on experimental and analysis tasks, data sharing, joint operation of computer and instrument resources, and exchange of personal expertise.

A number of articles have described the technology and implementation of Collaboratories (Kouzes, 1995, 1996, 1997). This chapter summarizes these technology developments, discusses implementation of a collaboratory, and more deeply explores the social issues of electronic collaboration.

THE COLLABORATORY AS A "PLACE"

A collaboratory is created to facilitate scientific interaction within a team by creating a new, artificial environment in which individuals can interact (Fig. 5.1). Many computing tools must be brought together and integrated to allow seamless interaction. Some of these tools are already in wide use, such as electronic mail and the World Wide Web, while others, like tele-presence, are still being created by researchers. This new "place" must be socially acceptable to the people who participate, and it must improve their ability to work. If the work process is not perceived to be significantly improved, people will not make the effort to overcome the energy barrier of working through a new technology system. Hesiod, circa 700 B.C., said that "first came chaos." Mankind has attempted to bring order from this chaos, and science has brought

FIG. 5.1. Collaboratories utilize communications technology to tie researchers from disparate locations together to enable more effective collaborative science. Resources are shared among multiple sites, making more effective use of instruments and collaborators.

logic to the process. Most people do not like either complexity or change, but those that thrive on chaos will lead the next scientific industrial age.

Scientific collaborations, large and small, currently rely heavily on face-to-face interactions, group meetings, individual action, and hands-on experimentation. Through immersive electronic interaction, the tools of computer supported cooperative work (CSCW) provide the ability for teams in widespread locations to collaborate using the newest instruments and computing resources. Capabilities such as shared secure data, shared analysis, shared instruments, and shared interaction spaces needed to facilitate science impose a number of functional requirements on collaboratory systems. Providing access to scientific instruments and collaborators from distance locations is one common driver for collaboratory development.

A number of both commercial and research software tools and integrated systems have been developed to allow electronic collaboration. Tools utilized include: audio/video conferencing, text chat boxes, shared computer display capability, electronic notebooks, file sharing, online instruments, computational resources, common visualizations, shared whiteboards, and World Wide Web browser synchronization. Commercial software systems, available from Sun, SGI, IBM, HP and others, provide fully integrated environments of such tools. The major limitation of these systems is the restriction to a single vendor hardware environment in most cases. In addition, all present technologies are limited by today's network bandwidth and by the ways that software interfaces with humans.

COLLABORATORY PROTOTYPES

Immersive data exploration tools with cognizance of human psychological needs have been developed that allow the user to sail through their data, allowing a deep and rapid understanding of its nature. Molecular biologists are pooling their knowledge of gene sequences and gene maps by establishing and maintaining large databases. Space physicists and oceanographers share their data (Cerf, 1993.) Some of the collaboratory prototypes are listed in Table 5.1.

An advanced example of a data-driven collaboration is the Worm Community System, one of the original U.S. National Science Foundation (NSF) sponsored collaboratory projects (Schatz, 1992). This system supports researchers studying the nematode *C. elegans*, which is a harmless, soil-residing worm of little human significance. It provides a repository for data spanning the spectrum from genome to behavior, and ties this data to the literature, including journals, newsletters, and informal notes. Everything known about *C. elegans* and everyone contributing to this knowledge is accessible through the system. These capabilities elevate the Worm Community System from a simple tool for sharing data to an electronic forum that creates a "worm community."

TABLE 5.I

Selected Collaboratory Projects

Collaboratory	Science	Http URL WWW Address
BioMOO	Biology	bioinfo.weizmann.ac.il:8888
Distributed Collaboratory Experiment Environments	Physics	www-itg.lbl.gov/DCEEpage/DCEE_Overview.html
DOE 2000 Projects	Physics	www.mcs.anl.gov/DOE2000
Diesel Collaboratory	Combustion	www-collab.ca.sandia.gov/Diesel
EMSL Collaboratory	Environment	www.emsl.pnl.gov:2080/docs/collab
InterMed	Medicine	smi.stanford.edu/projects/intermed-web
Microscopic Digital Anatomy	Biology	www-ncmir.ucsd.edu/CMDA
Remote Experiment Environment	Fusion	www.fusionscience.org/collab/REE
UARC	Atmospheric	www.si.umich.edu/UARC/HomePage.html

These projects are examples of implementations of collaboratories for various scientific purposes.

Providing access to scientific instruments from distant locations, one central component of remote experimentation, is another common driver for Collaboratories. Early work has focused on large, expensive instruments such as astronomical telescopes, particle accelerators, oceanographic instruments, atmospheric observatories, and space research applications. An example of remote experimentation is the Upper Atmospheric Research collaboratory (UARC), another of the NSF collaboratory projects, which provides access for half a dozen institutions to instruments sited in Greenland for observation of the solar wind. The UARC collaborators exchange and archive multimedia information from the instruments and their analysis of the measurements.

Recently, hundreds of smaller instruments such as nuclear magnetic resonance systems, electron microscopes and scanning tunneling microscopes have been remote-enabled (Cassidy, 1993; Mercurio, 1992). These latter applications are more typical of the applications in many areas of physics and chemistry. Remote experimentation, or tele-experimentation, is central to the collaboratory needs in the physical and environmental sciences.

In the area of medicine, there have also been significant advances in applying collaborative tools. The military have invested heavily in tele-medicine technology and have deployed systems to such locations as Somalia and Haiti. Tele-medicine provides for remote diagnosis and consultation between surgeons, and opens the possibility for surgery using robotics controlled remotely by a surgeon with mechanical manipulators. There are many programs used in the field of telemedicine that provide video conferencing, whiteboard, and image sharing capabilities (Burrow, Toler, Pelfer, Sinclair, & Gadacz, 1994; Martinez & Chimiak, 1994). The military are striving to develop the capability to use remotely controlled robotics to deliver the best surgical skill to the battlefield during the "golden hour" after trauma. To succeed, the surgeon will need immersive visual, tactile, acoustic and olfactory feedback—a technological challenge presently being tackled. A recent demonstration of a complex national tele-medicine implementation for the U.S. Congress showed the benefit of nationwide access to patient records, universal patient identification, telemetry of radiological information, and tele-consultation, while pointing out the legal hindrances of state licensure and insurance claim restrictions.

The BioMOO developed at the Weizmann Institute is a collaborative environment for biological science. The BioMOO exists in cyberspace as a meeting place for biological researchers. The term MOO (MUD, Object Oriented) derives from MUD (Multiple User Dialogue or Multiple User Dungeon), a concept developed largely at Xerox PARC, and is navigated via text commands. While navigating through the BioMOO, one encounters bulletin boards, seminars, and other individuals. This virtual meeting place provides a new interaction paradigm for science, and graphical versions of scientific MOOs are on the horizon.

HISTORY, GOALS, AND ORGANIZATION OF THE ENVIRONMENTAL SCIENCES COLLABORATORY

The U.S. Department of Energy (DOE) must deal with a legacy of environmental contamination and chemical and radioactive waste left from the U.S. nuclear weapons program. This environmental problem spans dozens of sites throughout the United States. DOE has an environmental problem of a magnitude only exceeded by the weapons production related contamination in the former Soviet Union. Over half of DOE's environmental problems exist at the Hanford Site in southeastern Washington state, where plutonium was produced and separated for weapons, starting with the first nuclear explosion at the Trinity site in New Mexico in July 1945 and the Nagasaki weapon of the same year, through the Reagan administration of the mid 1980s. The DOE's commitment to environmental cleanup at its sites presents significant scientific and technical challenges. These challenges are exemplified by the environmental problems at Hanford, more than 560 square miles in area, which has approximately 1.4 cubic kilometers of hazardous and radioactive wastes, 150 square miles of contaminated aquifer, 60 millions gallons of radioactive wastes (260 MCi) stored in underground storage tanks (of which more than one-third are believed to be leaking), 270 tons of spent fuel, 9 inactive reactors, and 7 major inactive reprocessing plants.

To deal with the huge environmental mess left from weapons development and testing, DOE has created an Environmental Molecular Sciences Laboratory (EMSL), a 200,000-square-foot, $230 million research facility recently completed at Pacific Northwest National Laboratory (PNNL). The EMSL is to be a national focus for the environmental and molecular science research communities. The EMSL's resources enable scientists to apply advanced capabilities to research and technology development in areas such as contaminated soils and groundwater; waste analysis, characterization, processing, and storage; and human and ecological health effects. The EMSL is also part of DOE's high-performance computing network linked to the other national laboratories, and to universities and industrial laboratories, allowing data and information generated in the EMSL to be shared electronically with the national and international scientific communities. As a national collaborative research and technology laboratory, the EMSL attracts scientists from academia, industry, and other government laboratories across the United States and around the world.

Environmental science is characteristic of many multidisciplinary research disciplines. The nature of environmental research is inherently collaborative—scientists with expertise in chemistry, materials science, condensed matter physics, molecular biology, and environmental science must work together to address complex environmental problems. In the long term, the success of the DOE's environmental research will be judged in cross-disciplinary terms, by how well and how efficiently hazardous waste sites can be made safe and restored to productive use.

Starting in 1993, the author initiated a project to create the first collaboratory within DOE, thereby making the EMSL more effective as a nationally accessible, collaborative, basic environmental sciences research center. The goal of implementing a collaboratory for the EMSL was to take the first major step in making true national environmental sciences teamwork possible through providing access to the resources of the EMSL independent of geographical location. A collaboratory Workshop was held at PNNL in March 1994 to begin the development of the collaboratory. Following this workshop, the author organized a team of chemists, physicists, computer scientists, engineers, and sociologists to create the collaboratory systems, software and environment. The project was organized as a multi-department, matrixed team. The collaboratory was initially supported from the EMSL project and Laboratory Discretionary Research and Development funds. The following year, competitive funding was obtained from DOE as part of the Distributed Collaboratory Experiment Environments (DCEE) program.

The EMSL collaboratory development continues at PNNL (now under the leadership of Dr. James Myers) with the evolution of improved software tools and systems. Work is funded for development of new electronic notebooks, a common software bus for supporting collaboration tools, and the general development of the shared collaborative environment for supporting scientific research. The collaboratory will make the EMSL an effective national user facility for environmental research.

COLLABORATORY PROTOTYPES
IN THE NATIONAL LABORATORIES

Researchers in the US Department of Energy National Laboratories (Table 5.2) initiated a series of collaboratory projects known as the Distributed Collaboratory Experiment Environments (DCEE) program. The four projects making up DCEE were:

TABLE 5.2
Multiprogram National Laboratories

National Laboratory	Location	Notable Facility
Argonne National Laboratory	Illinois	Advanced Photon Source
Brookhaven National Laboratory	New York	National Light Source
Lawrence Berkeley National Laboratory	California	Advanced Light Source
Lawrence Livermore National Laboratory	California	Combustion Research Center
Los Alamos National Laboratory	New Mexico	Advanced Computing Laboratory
Oak Ridge National Laboratory	Tennessee	Hollifield Accelerator
Pacific Northwest National Laboratory	Washington	EMSL
Sandia National Laboratory	New Mexico	Agile Manufacturing Prototyping

DOE manages over 30 laboratories, among them are the multiprogram National Laboratories listed above. These facilities, each funded at an annual level of from $200M to over $1B, contain a wide array of scientific research instrumentation and expertise. It is this type of capability that DOE hopes to make more widely available through a virtual laboratory approach using Collaboratory technology.

- Argonne National Laboratory, together with Northeastern University, is building and testing "LabSpace: A National Electronic Laboratory Infrastructure." A shared space with persistence and history is being implemented in two application testbeds. One is the Telepresence Electron Microscopy project, allowing remote use of the Advanced Analytical Electron Microscope and the Analytical Scanning Electron Microscope. The second involves a collaboration at CERN, the European high-energy physics center that will exercise the LabSpace version of a collaboratory in a larger collaboration spanning an international data link.

- Fusion energy R&D is an archetype of research that must be carried out at a few large central facilities. This will be particularly true in the next generation of experiments that rely on international participation, and are being designed for steady-state operation, for which interactive, real-time experimentation becomes an important issue. These challenges have brought together Lawrence Livermore National Laboratory, Oak Ridge National Laboratory, the Princeton Plasma Physics Laboratory, and General Atomics who are conducting remote operations at the D-IIID tokamak fusion facility. This project, "Distributed Computing Testbed for a Remote Experimental Environment," demands not only real-time synchronization and exchange of data among multiple computer networks, but also the presentation of sufficient auditory and visual information associated with the control room environment so that remote staff at multiple sites can be fully integrated in operations.

- The University of Wisconsin-Milwaukee will remotely operate a sophisticated synchrotron radiation beamline in "The SpectroMicroscopy Laboratory at the Advanced Light Source." This collaboratory development project allows remote access to three analytical tools at the Advanced Light Source located at Lawrence Berkeley National Laboratory to provide spatially resolved chemical information at length scales ranging from one micron down to the atomic scale. The collaboration that uses these instruments is fairly large and geographically distributed, with investigators from nine institutions, so the potential for saving the time and expense of training, staffing, and travel is considerable. One particularly interesting target audience for remote usage of this and similar facilities is the semiconductor industry, which has a critical need for sample inspection.

- Pacific Northwest National Laboratory is working on "Collaboratory Development in the Environmental and Molecular Sciences." The testbed is based on instrumentation being developed for the EMSL project, specifically, two unique nuclear magnetic resonance spectrometers, which are large, highly shared items, and some small instruments used by a limited number of researchers in molecular-beam reaction dynamics. Thus the characteristics of two related yet distinct scientific cultures, working with two quite different kinds of machines, are being examined.

DOE has made a major commitment to developing the technology to create a virtual laboratory system encompassing the vast scientific resources of the national laboratories, enabling greater participation by scientists around the world in solving DOE's science and technology challenges. DOE has recently begun a new series of collaboratory projects under the DOE2000 Program, which is emphasizing research in collaboratory tools plus industrial collaboration in collaboratory pilot projects. Among the funded DOE2000 collaboratory research activities are:

- The Collaboratory Interoperability Framework project will produce a distributed computing software bus that is required to support development of scientific collaboratories, will coordinate tool integration from other R&D projects, and will develop a common communication library including both multicast and unicast. Argonne National Laboratory, Lawrence Berkeley National Laboratory, Pacific Northwest National Laboratory, and Sandia National Laboratory are collaborating on this effort. The Collaboratory Interoperability Framework will allow scientific instruments, notebooks, and real-time collaboration tools to work together. At PNNL, the collaboratory development team has begun investigating ways to use the Common Object Request Broker Architecture (CORBA) in its electronic notebook development project and in its CORE2000 session management software. A Lightweight Directory Access Protocol (LDAP) Directory Server receives information from the registration webpage and then provide background information on real-time session participants and notebook authors. Investigations are also underway on methods to secure and encrypt communications for remote instruments and collaborative tools.

- The Electronic Logbooks project will develop a modular, extensible notebook framework and use it to produce cross-platform interoperating prototype implementations based on modern object-oriented design. Lawrence Berkeley National Laboratory, Pacific Northwest National Laboratory, and Oak Ridge National Laboratory are collaborating on this project. The Electronic Notebook system provides a sharable, multimedia version of the traditional paper scientific notebook. A Memorandum of Understanding has been signed with the Collaborative Electronic Notebook Systems Association (CENSA), a group of Chemical and Pharmaceutical companies promoting commercial electronic notebooks, to allow the DOE2000 notebook project and CENSA to share information on electronic notebook requirements and design. The notebook group has also decided on an "editor" application programming interface that allows third parties to add new data types into notebooks without rewriting the notebook engine or client.

- The Collaborative Session Management project will create persistent representations of sessions and people that include audio/video conferencing, shared electronic notebooks, and electronic whiteboard tools. It will develop and integrate tools for real-time collaboration, from video conferencing and display sharing to collaborative scientific instruments. This is under development by Argonne National Laboratory and Pacific Northwest National Laboratory. The Collaborative Session Management project has licensed the National Center for Supercomputing Applications' Habanero environment and has integrated video conferencing tools and the EMSL TeleViewer into a package that is available from the EMSL collaboratory page. A multiple whiteboard tool that helps manage multiple shared and private whiteboards was developed by a graduate student from West Virginia University and is part of the distribution.

- Shared Virtual Spaces are under development at Argonne National Laboratory to address existing barriers to deploying shared virtual reality spaces for the output of simulations and rendering of experimental data.

- A Scalable Security Architecture is being defined by Lawrence Berkeley National Laboratory to demonstrate a general and modular security architecture that will address the goal of protecting open network applications while providing flexible interfaces to enable cross-platform, cross-component implementations of the architecture with security functions.

- A bandwidth broker application is being developed by Lawrence Berkeley National Laboratory to provide Quality of Service that will become part of the administrative hierarchy to manipulate the bandwidth allocation machinery in order to provide sustained bandwidth for an application.

- Floor control mechanisms are being integrated into the Mbone tool architecture by Lawrence Berkeley National Laboratory so that it is possible to have moderated meetings during video conferencing.

- A Collaboration Management Environment will develop a real-time collaboration framework to integrate existing but incompatible collaboration tools, and will develop two user interfaces. This work is being done at Argonne National Laboratory and Pacific Northwest National Laboratory.

In addition to these research activities, the DOE2000 program includes two pilot Collaboratories that will use the technologies developed in the research efforts. The Diesel Combustion collaboratory is exploring diesel engine emissions control. The partners in this project are Sandia National Laboratory, Lawrence Berkeley National Laboratory, Lawrence Livermore National Laboratory, the University of Wisconsin, Cummins Engine Company, Caterpillar Inc., and Detroit Diesel. The Materials MicroCharacterization Collaboratory is investigating the microstructure of technologically advanced materials, with focus on interface characterization for a wide user community. The partners in this project include Oak Ridge National Laboratory, Lawrence Berkeley National Laboratory, Argonne National Laboratory, the National Institute of Standards and Technology, the University of Illinois, Gatan, Inc., EMiSPEC Systems Inc., Philips Electronic Instruments, Hitachi Scientific Instruments, and Japan Electron Optics Laboratories USA.

SUPPORTING ELECTRONIC COLLABORATION

Electronic collaboration in a collaboratory goes beyond the traditional file sharing and e-mail, and beyond the current videoconferencing paradigm, to reach the level where collaborators work intimately with one another. Collaboratory implementations are built on an integrated set of cross-platform tools (Table 5.3), including electronic notebooks, video conferencing, electronic whiteboards, shared screens, information access tools, instrument control tools, and others. Collectively they create an electronic meeting place for the interaction among scientific teams; as such they must be cognizant of the sociology of science and human nature.

Software tools for collaborative work are used in varying ways as seen in Fig. 5.2. Some tools are synchronous in nature, while others are synchronous. Some work well for more static applications, while some are inherently dynamic. For example, an electronic whiteboard tends to be used synchronously between collaborators in dynamic interactions, although it may also be retained as an archival document, or may be a prepared static slide for use in an presentation. A shared screen (televiewer) will almost always be a synchronous and dynamic tool to allow interactive shared windows between collaborators. The role of a tool in a collaboration may evolve as the collaboration matures.

Electronic mail supports collaboration via a time serial dialog. Videoconferencing supports real-time discussion and, with the addition of graphics and whiteboard capabilities, presentation and brainstorming. The collaboratory concept brings the scientific resources used by researchers, including instruments, high performance computers, data analysis, visualization, and modeling applications, archival data including lab notes, and the

TABLE 5.3

Software Tools for Supporting Collabotory Science

Audio/video Conferencing	Audio/video conferencing allows collaborators to see and hear each other, as well as to monitor instruments and laboratories. Network based software, such as the Mbone, are the main tools being used in DOE projects.
Chat Box	Text messaging.
Shared Computer Displays	This tool allows users to view and interact with any program running on the shared display, including word processors, spreadsheets, instrument control software, and scientific computations, simulations, and visualizations. Whiteboard style annotation on top of the live image and the ability to remotely control the shared application are two types of interaction possible. This tool allows non-collaborative applications to be used collaboratively.
Shared Electronic Notebook	Electronic notebooks provide users with a shared version of the traditional paper laboratory notebook. In addition to distributed access, which benefits the group, the electronic notebook provides automated data entry, searching, and other information processing capabilities not possible with a paper notebook that add value for the individual researcher and research team alike.
File Sharing	Drag and drop transfer of files between multiple collaborators.
On-line Instruments, Computation, and Visualization	Data acquisition, analysis, computation, and visualization software that was written for a single, local user, can be modified to be used collaboratively in an environment such as CORE.
Shared Whiteboard	Whiteboards augment videoconferencing by providing a shared space where users can write and draw.
WWW Browser Synchronization	Synchronization of web browsers allows users to hold lectures or discussions, using material on the WWW. When one user goes to a new URL, all linked browsers automatically go to the new document. Lecture (only the leader's browser is echoed) or discussion (peer-to-peer) modes are possible.

Such tools are included in those used in the EMSL Collaboratory project.

scientific literature into the mix for collaborative use. Both real-time work and synchronous collaboration are possible. The effect of having all scientific resources available to all researchers moves a remote collaborator into the role of a true coworker.

An example of an integrated environment for collaboration is CORE, developed as part of the EMSL DCEE program, a prototype for an environment that provides a loosely integrated set of internet based collaborative capabilities that appear to collaborators as extensions to the World Wide Web. CORE provides a simple "one click" method to start or join multi-tool collaborative

Static	Telementoring	Information Browsing

A
u
d
i
o

V
i
d
e
o

Web Browser

White board

Shared Screens

Electronic Notebook

Email

Dynamic   Teleconferencing   Shared Work

Synchronous   Asynchronous

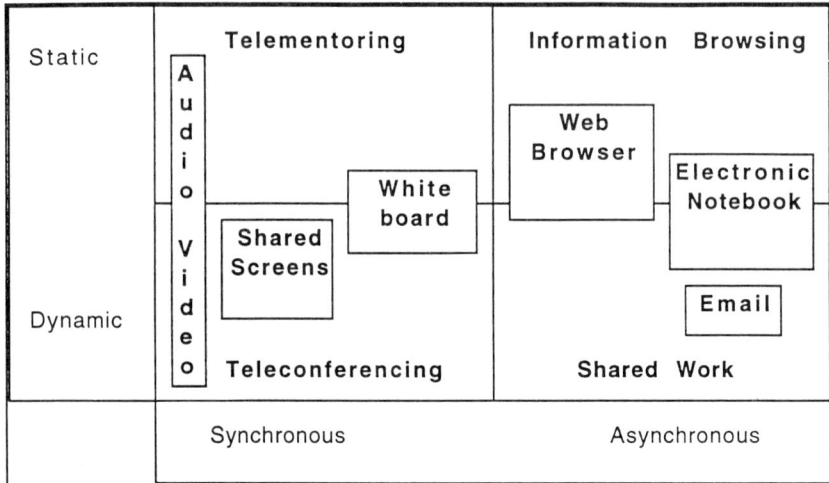

FIG. 5.2. Tools provide varying functionality for a collaborative interaction. Some tools are synchronous in nature, whereas others are asynchronous. Some work well for more static applications, whereas some are inherently dynamic. The role of a tool in a collaboration may evolve as the collaboration matures.

sessions from a web page. The web is central to the current development of collaboratory tools because it provides a uniformly accessible interface to all collaborators.

The CORE session manager and desktop executive launch and track active sessions, participants, and tools, giving users the ability to pick collaborative capabilities appropriate for their work without awareness of the connection syntax of individual tools, or of port numbers, firewalls, or their collaborators' internet addresses. The cross-platform (unix, mac, windows compatible) nature of these tools is a central requirement because dispersed collaborators usually have a variety of desktop platforms. Some of the capabilities available (or under development) through these tools are shown in Table 5.3. Recent developments of the CORE have utilized new collaborative middleware software such as Habanera from NCSA to provide the facilitation and synchronization of the shared tools.

The integration of these tools into a usable, integrated, user friendly, software environment with cognizance of the users psychosocial needs is required. Fig. 5.3 shows an example of an integrated collaboratory software environment using a whiteboard, electronic notebook, chat box, tele-viewer, information browser, and video conferencing. This present tool set is a realization using today's applications, and is rapidly evolving as more is being

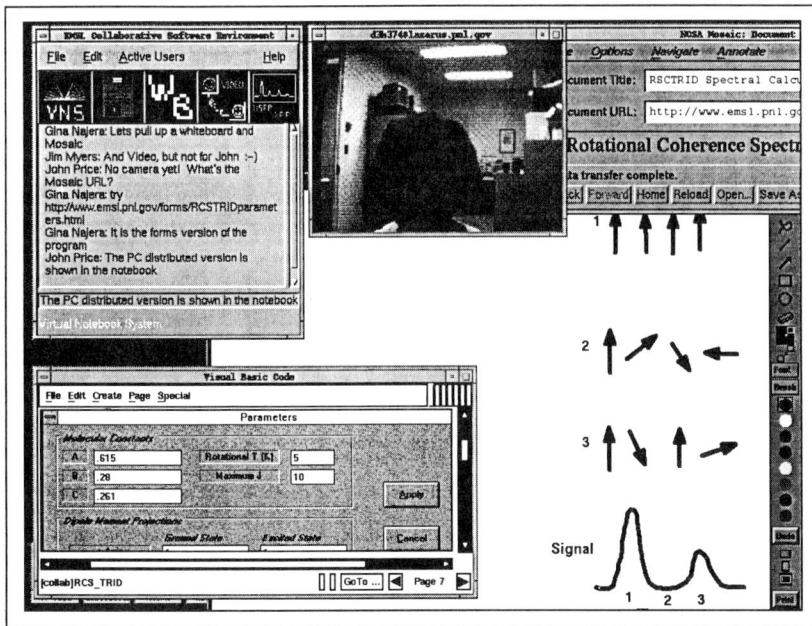

FIG. 5.3. An integrated Collaboratory software environment uses software tools such as whiteboards, electronic notebooks, chat boxes, tele-viewers, information browsers, and video conferencing to facilitate effective interactions between dispersed scientists. This present tools set is a realization using today's applications, and is rapidly evolving as more is being learned about facilitating the collaborative process. The example shown is an early version of the integrated environment developed as part of the EMSL Collaboratory initiative.

learned about facilitating the collaborative process. The example shown is an early version of the integrated environment developed as part of the EMSL collaboratory initiative.

THE SOCIOLOGY OF COLLABORATION

Science is a complex intertwining of creativity, discovery, and interpretation that builds a body of truth from fragments of knowledge learned through the research process. Collaboration is at the heart of science. The renowned scientist Sir Isaac Newton said "If I have seen further, it is by standing on the shoulders of giants." The collaborations found in scientific research are carried out with a tradition spanning many decades, if not centuries. As the power of information technologies has grown, it has brought humans to the threshold of a strange, new collaboratory setting. In this synthetic place, distributed across space and time yet maintained through loops of electronic information flow, individuals will convene, converse, and cooperate on some of the most challenging scientific problems of the 21st century. Jim Wise of PNNL declared that "the Collaboratory concept is nothing less than the village square and campfire juxtaposed to the Information Age."

The 1990s experience with communication via electronic systems revealed the ubiquity and usefulness of human social controls that go mostly unnoticed in face-to-face contacts. When a technical medium of discourse removes these controls, their role becomes apparent. The first language of control is gesture; and every social encounter takes place in the context of this silent language of body motions and spatial positions. Body orientation and movement, the interpersonal speaking distance, and making and breaking of eye contact all send silent messages that are just as meaningful as the spoken word. These are the means that maintain social controls on spoken exchanges, and yet they are absent in the electronic medium.

In terms of the written word, e-mail is the great communications leveler. A person who would never think of calling a complete stranger to ask for assistance with a reference or a technical problem will have no compunction in contacting that stranger via e-mail. E-mail also often omits the obligatory social salutations and closing rituals that mark personal correspondence or telecommunications. The silent, social controls of personal discourse are uniformly absent in e-mail. *Emoticons* or *smileys*, a set of symbol characters to be read sideways as a facial pictogram, have only recently appeared as a way to convey feelings in an unfeeling medium, {:-).

Even when the image and sound of a person is restored through audio/video communications, technical limitations can make the exchange much less than satisfying. Improper placement of a pickup camera can make it appear disconcertingly that the speaker is always looking away from the listener. Limited bandwidth in picture transmission can produce freeze frames that catch the individual in the middle of a sneeze, yawn, or eye blink. The small size and placement of monitors can promote a talking heads impression that socially diminishes the messenger and the message.

Groupware computer applications have been aimed at a variety of purposes such as meeting schedulers, group decision support, joint authorship, and distributed management. and have had a decidedly checkered history. The failure of groupware to gain wide acceptance has come from its primitive technology and a lack of understanding of the intended user's workplace, including insensitivity to social and political issues. Groupware has also suffered from the misconception that its implementation is akin to single user applications, although it demands a different role in an organization. Groupware applications for a collaboratory will have to be selected and implemented with a clear understanding of the social and political concerns that characterize joint scientific work. Among these are issues of authorship, acknowledgment of contributions, esteem of peers, and recognition by professional role models.

Can participants who find a need for remote collaboration adapt to this synthetic collaboratory place? The 1933 Chicago World's Fair had the motto: "Science finds, industry applies, man conforms." It is clear that such a technocentric belief is incompatible with today's expectations. A collaboratory must consider psychosocial issues such as autonomy, a sense of place, attention to ritual, and engendering a sense of trust (Table 5.4). Translating such abstract psychological factors into practice with today primitive computing tools is the main barrier to widespread adoption of collaboratory methodology in science. Instead, we must rely on limited implementations with individuals who are sufficiently motivated to overcome the frequent technology problems to reach their science goals.

Autonomy describes how an organization is governed or regulated, and is implemented through informal communications, acquaintances, and associations that occur in any organization. Autonomy within a collaboratory must be imbedded in a considered manner into the virtual organization. Trust is established among collaborators through shared experience. A collaboratory will have to engage some special means to establish the sort of trust that co-workers normally develop over time through informal means by meeting face-to-face and working together in the same place. A sense of place allows people to feel comfortable in their surroundings, providing security in which to be creative. The Disney theme parks are perhaps the most inclusively and thoroughly designed settings on the planet that create a wonderfully unique and magical sense of place that delights young and old. If a collaboratory can harness some of the design strategies that have been so successful in physical group settings, it can also create a sense of place and purpose among its dispersed members that will engender an enduring sense of affiliation and cooperation toward its goals. A collaboratory environment must provide the richness of information to allow for such natural interactions among collaborators.

TABLE 5.4

Psychosocial Issues Crucial to the Success of a Collaboratory

Attention to ritual	Allows for the required mechanisms of social interaction
Autonomy	Determines how an organization is governed or regulated
Sense of place	Allows people to feel comfortable in their surroundings
Sense of trust	Allows people to cooperatively interact

Dealing with psychosocial issues is crucial to the success of a collaboratory. Creating an electronic place where issues, including these four, are considered will allow humans to work collaboratively.

Although psychosocial issues are not science specific, success in addressing such human factors is the limiting element in creating a successful collaboratory implementation.

EVALUATION OF COLLABORATORY TECHNOLOGY

As part of the EMSL collaboratory development, evaluations have been done of the effectiveness of the collaborative computing tools and sociological issues of collaboration. Much can be learned about the process of scientific collaboration from discussions with scientists themselves. Scientific collaborations span a wide range in terms of group size, collaboration style, and focus (experimental, theoretical, computational), even within a single research facility. The EMSL houses many unique facilities for basic scientific research, including the world's first commercial gigahertz Nuclear Magnetic Resonance spectrometer, and the most powerful IBM parallel supercomputer yet built, as well as many smaller instruments with unique capabilities from benchtop electrochemistry instruments to laser systems and mass spectroscopy tools. The EMSL will house nearly 300 researchers with unique expertise, equipment, and software.

As part of the initial EMSL collaboratory software development efforts, researchers were asked about the nature of their current and future collaborations in order to understand the diversity of communications an electronic collaborative environment must support. Collaborative interactions fall into the four following categories.

Peer-to-Peer Collaboration

Some collaborations involve researchers in the same field sharing an instrument. The remote researcher might contribute to the design of a new detector and then use the instrument to study systems of interest. In this peer-to-peer type of collaboration, the researchers share a common scientific vocabulary. The most important aspects of their collaborations are shared instruments and raw, unanalyzed data, making remote instrument control and direct data file access important.

Mentor–Student Collaboration

A second type of collaboration is between senior scientists and their more junior partners, (e.g., students). In these mentor–student collaborations, the mentor may use prepared materials and live demonstrations to teach a student data acquisition or analysis techniques, or to convey scientific principles. The mentor then observes as the student demonstrates mastery of the new concepts. The real-time interactions between mentor and student go far beyond standard conferencing; they must be able to work collaboratively and interactively directly with the data acquisition, analysis, visualization, simulation, and other specialized programs used in their experiments.

Interdisciplinary Collaboration

Related to this mentoring collaboration is one involving scientists doing complimentary, interdisciplinary studies of the same systems. For instance, a theorist may calculate the molecular structure of clusters while an experimentalist uses laser spectroscopy to make experimental structure measurements. Researchers in such collaborations share less of a common vocabulary and must often translate their results into each other's terms. They alternate between the roles of mentor and student as they seek to synthesize their respective findings. Direct access to instruments and raw data are less useful to these researchers, while access to summaries and analyses, perhaps recorded into an electronic notebook, and the ability to easily discuss unfamiliar concepts and to correct misunderstandings, become more important.

Producer–Consumer Collaboration

A fourth type of collaboration, again involving researchers in different disciplines, involves one researcher, or research team, providing input for another. Examples of this type of collaboration include a mass spectroscopist determining the sequence of a protein for a biologist, or a surface scientist providing reaction rate data, to a geologist modeling the subsurface transport of hazardous wastes. Working with an analytical laboratory on a fee-per-service basis represents an extreme form of this producer–consumer type of collaboration. There is often a wider gap between the disciplines and motivations of researchers in such collaborations; a scientist may be interested in a new physical phenomenon while an engineering collaborator is trying to reduce the cost of a clean up effort. They may have little chance for professional contact in their daily work or at conferences. Researchers in these types of relationships place the strongest emphasis on being able to receive a sample, and then transmitting results back to the other party. However, new ideas and approaches can appear if these researchers communicate more closely.

An individual collaboration may actually contain elements from several of these interaction styles, either in parallel, or as the collaboration evolves. The categorizations help to show the varying communications needs researchers have as they work in different modes, and how an individual researcher's needs may change based on the task at hand or the nature of the collaboration.

The fact that researchers may switch collaboration styles frequently as they work through various tasks in an experiment implies that an electronic collaboratory environment should not impose a particular mode of interaction. It should instead provide a wide range of capabilities that can be selected quickly and easily, and configured, for the task at hand. Such flexibility addresses some of the social barriers inhibiting collaboration.

LESSONS LEARNED AND CHALLENGES TO THE ADOPTION OF COLLABORATORY TECHNOLOGY

Collaboratory implementation faces both technical and sociological barriers. The software tools that exist today for deploying collaboratories are immature, lacking in integration, challenging to support, and costly to maintain. Collaboratories rely on the development of sophisticated software and hardware to create the electronic environment through which a scientific collaboration occurs. The sophistication required by a collaboratory system as envisioned for the future is far from what can be delivered today. Attaining this future vision will require years of effort and a significant investment by government and industry. In addition, there will be many false starts along with the occasional successes. After all, we know that only 16% of software projects are finished on time and on budget (94% of software projects are restarted at least once and 33% of all project are canceled). Software projects are known to fail because of the lack of user input, which is a special challenge for systems as complex as a collaboratory.

The concept of richer, multimedia interaction between remote individuals has been with us for a long time. An example of the technological challenge can be found in the 1914 fictional book *Tom Swift and His Photo Telephone*, where Barton Swift says to his son "It can't be done Tom! ... This thing of sending a picture over a telephone wire is totally out of the question, and entirely opposed to all the principles of science" (Appleton, 1914). This book describes the use of video teleconferencing. Technology often exists without being utilized because it is not perceived as adding value to a process. Although we contend that the time is right for a collaboratory solution to the needs of scientific interaction, we are challenged to make it a viable necessity for scientific progress.

In the area of video-conferencing technology, a number of systems have become available in the late 1990s, with a disappointing market response (Machrone, 1994). The explanation for the slow adoption of these systems lies partly in the cost, hardware restrictions, lack of standards, and poor video quality (Garland & Rowell, 1994). The greatest problem may be that there is not enough perceived benefit to be gained from video-conferencing to put up with the trouble of utilizing the presently available systems. The Mbone network based freeware applications used by many DOE collaboratory efforts for video-conferencing originated only in 1992 (Eriksson, 1994). The Mbone is utilized extensively by a small class of Internet users for video-conferencing and for the network based broadcast of meetings. The Unix based Mbone video applications typically provide frame rates of a few per second, while consuming about 200 kbytes/sec of network bandwidth. CuSeeMe, a freeware product from Cornell University, provides Macintosh and pc Windows access to video. Performance improvements are required in network video software for wider utilization to be realized for this technology.

One major challenge for collaboratory development is network bandwidth. Video creates the greatest bandwidth demand, whereas most other application require only modest bandwidth, including screen sharing mechanisms that can use change updating to minimize network needs. A problem arises from the explosion in world network demand, which can make remote collaboration unpredictable with regard to responsiveness. As of January 1997, 2% of the world population used the internet, with 16% of those over age 15 having access. In 1998 there were 16 million Internet hosts serving 57 million people in 194 countries. This exponentially growing demand will cause network saturation at many sites. One solution suggested to deal with this problem is restricted access networks like the NSF vBNS project. However, this concept cannot guarantee that all collaborators will have the needed access.

Organizational issues such as security and institutional credit must be addressed. Collaboratories by their nature are open structures in order that people may naturally flow in and out of them in cyberspace. Security may be a major hindrance to the value brought about by creating a laboratory without walls. The protection of intellectual property and of physical facilities, and of the privacy of people and data, must be considered. We face many challenges in shaping the technology that exists to meet our needs to enable the collaboratory including changing the institutional barriers that may kill the process before it is allowed to nurture.

Collaboratories bring value to science through efficiency and created opportunity. Obtaining funding for collaboratory development is a challenge due to its multidisciplinary nature, because it cannot be compartmentalized as science or as pure computer science. Collaboratories cannot be sold for their value as cost saving mechanisms. However, through the formation of greater opportunity for collaboration, the efficient utilization of scarce physical research resources will be improved.

THE FUTURE

Yogi Berra once said "Prediction is difficult, especially about the future." In general, we are very poor in our ability to predict the future of technology in society, although a few visionaries have been uncanny in this regard. For example, H.G. Wells in his 1914 book *A World Set Free* (Wells, 1914) describes the creation and use of the atomic bomb by the 1950s, a prediction made at a time when fission was unknown. There are however many examples of poor foresight for the rapidity of change, such as the statement in the August 1948 *Science Digest* stating "Landing and moving around the moon offers so many serious problems for human beings that it may take science another 200 years to lick them." Despite this record, let me make a few predictions about the future of scientific collaboration.

In the sciences, virtual laboratories will exist in large numbers, encompassing most large facilities including all of the National Laboratories. The accessibility of online instruments will enhance the ability of researchers and students to participate, or at least be aware of, the latest research. This will reduce the numbers of disenfranchised scientists now residing in smaller colleges. The talented amateur scientist may again find ways to contribute to scientific inquiry and progress.

Multidisciplinary collaborations will become required in science. This is partly driven by the increasing difficulty of complex scientific problems, such as environmental studies, which require expertise from every field. The need for collaboration will also be pushed forward by new funding models for scientific research that are created by cooperation among funding sources necessitated by leveraging of declining budgets and political factors.

Additionally, we will be faced with managing increasing complexity in every aspect of our lives. Collaborations are inherently more complex than the individual researcher working alone in a laboratory. Because collaborations will be required in research, we will be seeking ways to create and manage them effectively. Collaboratories provide the technology for this structure.

It is clear that collaboratories have the potential to greatly benefit the scientific community by expanding the resources available to individual researchers, increasing the efficiency of our research system, and coupling basic to applied research efforts. We must appreciate at the same time that implementing information technology does not by itself improve or create a collaboration.

Some observers report that productivity improvements in corporate America have dropped in recent years since the introduction of computers in the workplace, and give this as an example of technology inhibiting human effectiveness. We must retain our awareness at every step of the collaboratory development process that psychosocial issues can be the dominant factor to success.

The current system of scientific communication via completed papers with occasional conferences and short visits has been with us since the 17th century. Despite the amazing advances in our technology to communicate rapidly and in great detail, there has been little change yet in the paradigm of scientific communication. Electronic mail and electronic publishing are forewarning a change to come, and web based scientific conferences are gaining popularity. The collaboratory concept is a qualitatively different way of using communication and information technologies. It has the potential to remove the walls around departments and organizations, and will lead to the creation of a meta-laboratory with capabilities that far exceed those available in any one laboratory alone.

ACKNOWLEDGMENTS

The work described in this article was partially supported by West Virginia University and the Laboratory Directed Research and Development program at Pacific Northwest National Laboratory. I especially recognize the contributions of Bill Wulf, Jim Myers, and Jim Wise. Further information on Collaboratories is available at http://www.wvu.edu/~research/.

REFERENCES

Appleton, V. (1914). *Tom Swift and his photo telephone*. New York: Grosset & Dunlap.

Burrow, M., Toler, J., Peifer, J., Sinclair, M., & Gadacz, T. (1994). A telemedicine testbed for developing and evaluating telerobotic tools for rural health care. In *Medicine meets virtual reality II* (pp. 15–17). San Diego, CA: Aligned Management Associates. (unedited compilation)

Cassidy, R. (1993). *Telemicroscopy: Dialing for better research & development*. New York: Cahners.

Cerf, V. G., Cameron, A. G. W., Lederberg, J., Russel, C. T., Schatz, B. R., Shames, P. M. B., Sproull, L. S., Weller, R. A., Wulf, W. A. (1993). *National collaboratories: Applying information technologies for scientific research*. Washington, DC: National Academy Press.

Eriksson, H. (1994). MBONE: The Multicast Backbone. *Communications of the Association for Computing Machines, 37*, 54–60.

Garland, E., & Rowell, D. (1994, November). Face to face collaboration. *Byte*, 233–242.

Imparato, N., & Harari, O. (1994). *Jumping the curve*. San Francisco, CA: Jossey-Bass.

Kouzes, R. T. (1997). Creating the cyberspace laboratory. In *The World & I* (March 1995) 190–197.

Kouzes, R. T. (1997). Collaboratories: Can we work together apart? *Scientific Computing and Automation, 14*, 52–54.

Kouzes, R. T., Myers, J. D., & Wulf W. A. (1996). Collaboratories: Doing science on the internet. *IEEE Computer, 29*, 40–46.

Machrone, W. (1994, June). Seeing is almost believing. *PC Magazine*, 233.

Martinez, R., & Chimiak, W. J. (Jan. 1994). Remote consultation and diagnosis via the global medical informatic consortium networks. In *Medicine meets virtual reality II* (pp. 140–143). San Diego, CA: Aligned Management Associates. (unedited compilation)

Mercurio, P. J., Elvins, T. T., Young, S. J., Cohen, P. S., Fau, K. R., Ellisman, M. H. (1992). The distributed laboratory: An interactive visualization environment for electron microscopy and three-dimensional imaging. *Communication of the ACM*, *35*(6), 54.

Schatz, B. R. (1992). Building an electronic community system. *Journal of Management Information Systems*, *8*(3), 87–107.

Wells, H. G. (1914). *A world set free*. New York: E. P. Dutton.

Wulf, W. A. (1989). The national collaboratory–A white paper. In *Towards a National collaboratory*. Unpublished report of a workshop held at Rockefeller University, New York.

6 ❖❖❖ Electronic Collaboration: Implications for Neurosciences

Floyd E. Bloom
Warren G. Young
The Scripps Research Institute

In recent years, progress in tools, concepts, and model systems in the neurosciences have not just been moving rapidly, but in fact at an accelerating pace. As a result, data are accumulating at rates far exceeding a scientist's normal ability to organize and recall. This trend in neuroscience informational overload continues today (Bloom, 1995; Bloom & Young, 1994). It is more difficult than ever to keep an ongoing and comprehensive overview of the scientific literature in any specialized discipline of the neurosciences. In fact, scientists now are beginning to recognize their loss of a broad awareness of new discoveries as they strive to retain their indepth awareness at best in only the most narrowly defined of fields. New enabling technologies, such as electronic communications, are part of the reason for the huge increase in scientific data. Computers, networks, the Web, electronic mail (e-mail), intelligent software, and software agents are making it easier than ever to transmit and receive data and information. However, if the present situation of informational overload is to be solved, it is these same enabling technologies that will have to provide the solution.

New social networks among communities of scientists, sometimes referred to as *collaboratories*, are developing as a use of these tools. Dr. William Wulf defined a collaboratory in 1993 as "a center without walls, in which the nations's researchers can perform their research without regard to geographical location—interacting with colleagues, accessing instrumentation, sharing data and computational resources, [and] accessing information in digital libraries." The simplest collaboratories might be scientists working together on common goals, but communicating data with the use of faxes or e-mails. Today, collaboratories might take full advantage of the Internet, sharing data electronically from desktop to desktop, and linking activities with video conferencing, data whiteboards, and common database repositories.

Neuroscience is not alone among active areas of biomedical science in recognizing the need for such information handling tools. For example, those several hundred scientists involved in the Human Genome Project (Cuticchia, Chiperfield, Porter, Keanns, & Pearson, 1993; Pearson & Söll, 1991) have acknowledged comparable problems with the acquisition, analysis, and sharing of information on an essentially linear, but extremely long two-dimensional dataset consisting of alternations in four nucleic acid bases. Although not diminishing their efforts, this is a far cry from the sorts of complexities to be faced in developing a brain information database. Nevertheless, despite the differences in the complexity of the information sets being studied, those involved in the Human Genome Project have been explicit in advocating for informatics investments, and have stated that "the success of the genome project will depend in large part on the ease with which biologists can gain access to and use the information produced." Therefore, increased emphasis on data handling, its organization, and its distribution remain major elements of the second 5 years of planning for the Human Genome Project.

Some fields of neurosciences will benefit directly from the information explosion. For example, the accelerated pace of molecular discovery has produced estimates that perhaps 97% of the Expressed Sequence Tags (ESTs) associated with the major brain genes of mice are already in hand (Mara, Thilier & Waterston, 1998). That progress means that there is an enormous backlog of preliminary information on gene expression patterns and potentially, some of the clues needed to link genes to neurons, neurons to circuits, and circuits to systems that underlie or regulate behavior. What are needed next are ways to link that sequence information with brain cellular and circuitry properties. That accomplishment would be a highly effective means to increase our knowledge about neuronal and glial phenotypes and about brain functions and diseases. However, there now exist no ways that are remotely as facile as the gene sequence comparison methods to determine how such genes map onto the independently growing base of information on the molecular, cellular, circuit, and systems of the brains of experimental animals and humans.

One may argue that the technological changes that are occurring in the computer and information industry are revolutionary. Desktop computers, networks, and novel software engineering have all but changed the way people think and work in many different fields. However, the changes that are occurring in the lives of neuroscientists have been more evolutionary than revolutionary. Even with all of the modern tools of information acquisition and analysis, there have been few changes to the basic way that neuroscientists work and communicate with each other. Scientists mainly still exchange information by reading journals and travelling to scientific meetings. This, despite the obvious recognition by all participants in the profession of neuroscience that the data they are reading or hearing are months to years behind the actual state of experimental progress at the bench tops of our field. The goal of this chapter is to show some of the progression in thinking that scientists have been making vis-à-vis new modes of electronic communication, and to discuss some of the efforts others, and our own group, have been making as part of this technological and sociological evolution.

EARLY FORMS OF ELECTRONIC COLLABORATION

In the late 1970s, scientists had a new and novel way to communicate with each other, other than picking up the telephone (Green, 1997). If you were fortunate to have a computer terminal on your desk, and you had a connection to some part of the Internet, which was then a government funded backbone of computers connected among major research institutions, you could send an electronic message to a colleague on another computer system. E-mail, as it was called, allowed for nearly instantaneous communication among scientists, and with the ease of typing the message into a computer. Once you had the mail message on your computer terminal, you could print it out, make some handwritten notes, or respond to it directly back to the sender. All of this opened up a new kind of collaboration. E-mail became the predominant messaging medium in the vast arena of prepublication of scientific inquiry (Harnad, 1990) where ideas and thoughts are tested against colleagues, where experiments producing the data are done, and where the data are laid out and measured against one another, which hopefully would lead to a scholarly publication. E-mail became a staple of the everyday scientific operation. Scientists depended on it as much as they did the phone or the postal mail system.

However, e-mail was no more than a messaging system. There are some kinds of data in science that simply cannot be represented by a message. For example, neuroanatomy and neuropathology traditionally have relied heavily on photography for the acquisition and display of data. For the scientist, the problem was how to get that kind of photographic information into the computer in some electronic form. In the 1970s, attaching a video camera to a computer was extremely difficult, and only the most proficient of laboratories had the knowledge, or the finances, to make digital images. Other types of data proved to be just as difficult to get into some digital form. Neurophysiologists routinely measured the electrical characteristics of neurons, but usually recorded the activity as analog recordings on tape. Printouts were made and measured and analyzed in the nondigital domain. Rarely would such data be moved into some form that could be encapsulated in a computer file so that it could be transmitted to another computer on a network. A/D and D/A converters were, like the video cameras and their digitizers, the provinces of the highly technical engineers.

Eventually, those barriers would be overcome. For neuroanatomists, systems that digitized real-time video into snapshots or captured some sort of reduced data that could be put into computer files, and for neurophysiologists, systems to convert electrophysiological data from analog into digital and back again, were becoming more mainstream (DuVarney & DuVarney, 1985; Lindsay, 1977; Part, 1985; Young, Morrison, & Bloom, 1985). With the growth of technology, the capacity for quantitative neuroanatomic analysis has increased substantially. The advent of better video technology and computer-assisted video microscopes with peripheral graphic capabilities made the computer invaluable when studying the distribution of cellular patterns across a tissue section. Modern graphics workstations and terminals connected to the computers permit unparalleled views into the data. Not only can the data be reconstructed into their inherent two-dimensional maps, but new views and insight may be synthesized by applying mathematical techniques to the numbers.

Eventually, all forms of laboratory systems began to develop around the technology. Computerized automatic densitometry systems have been developed (Agnati et al., 1984; Gallistel et al., 1982; Goochee, Resband, & Sokoloff, 1979; Hibbard & Hawkins, 1984; McEachron, Gallistel, Eilbert, & Tretiak, 1988; Mize, Holdefer, & Nabors, 1988; Palacios, Niehoff, & Kuhar, 1979; Toga & Arnicar-Sulze, 1987; Toga, Santori, & Samaie, 1986). Some computerized systems are designed to digitize or contour the outlines of cells or their fiber arborization (Eidelberg & Davis, 1977; Forbes & Petry, 1979; Glaser, Gissler, & Van der Loos, 1979; Woolsey & Dierker, 1978). Computer systems have also been designed to facilitate the reconstruction of structures from microscopes (Agnati et al., 1984; Capowski, 1977, 1983; Capowski & Rethelyi, 1978; Capowski & Sedivec, 1981; Macagno, Leventhal, & Sobel, 1979; McEachron et al., 1988; Nowakowski, 1989; Reuman & Capowski, 1984). And some computer systems can deal with reconstructions of larger sets of data, such as whole brain data (Capowski, 1977; Foote, 1980; Hillman, 1977; Toga et al., 1986).

All of these new computerized systems changed how the neurosciences were conducted in the laboratory, but they also were responsible for the development of new forms of data that could easily be represented by digital computer. For example, the field of view from the microscope could be represented by a byte-oriented image that represented spatial dots of each part of the field. Electrical activity from a cell could be recorded digitally as a linear sequence of scalars varying with time. However, it was not easy to send these data through e-mail. The size of the data files was generally very large, and many computers passing e-mail messages back and forth in the early 1980s had capacity limitations. Some mail systems also removed portions of the message that were not readable text, that is, conforming to the typed English alphabet. Digital images specifically would be damaged during transmission if affected in this manner. Other means of getting that data to a remote colleague were needed. One of the few other ways to move these files around was through the use of another network resource called File Transport Protocol (FTP). FTP was a service that was built into the mainstream operating systems of the 1970s, such as UNIX. With FTP, those data files could now be sent to and from other computer systems just as easily as the e-mail messages. In fact, FTP is data-insensitive. A text file describing some neuroanatomic finding can be transmitted and received just as easily as a binary file containing an image of a tissue section. The remote computer receives a perfect copy of the transmitted file. This proved to be an error-free way to send all kinds of information and data from one location to another. The word-processing file that contained a draft of the scientific manuscript or the file of the digitized image that pointed to some new finding could be on your collaborator's computer and desktop within seconds.

NEW MODES OF COMMUNICATION PROMOTE
NEW FORMS OF COLLABORATION

What does e-mail and FTP mean to the neuroscientist? New ways of doing science came about. Because your discovery could be viewed and delivered intact within seconds, new forms of collaborations began to emerge. A new concept of collaboratories began to develop where scientists flocked around common interests and goals, and linked themselves with modern communication techniques, such as e-mail and FTP (and other network services that are not discussed in this chapter). The clustering of scientists produced dependencies that did not exist before. The typical neuroscience laboratory became a cyber-lab, in a sense. The neurophysiologist who needs some expert neuroanatomical advice to locate his electrode placement after experimentation could consult electronically with his neuroanatomist colleague as part of the collaboratory. The image of the brain section could be sent immediately to a remote site, viewed on a microcomputer, and the place of the electrode could be determined by an expert, remotely, and communicated back to the original investigator with relative ease.

Scientists in the 1980s and early 1990s were slowly increasing their use of these new kinds of network services. They began to change their social behavior gradually from isolation or exclusively local collaborations into distant collaborative relationships which integrated these services into the way they do science. Meanwhile, other advances were being reached in the technology of computer telecommunications and were about to have another strong impact—the personal desktop computer.

PERSONAL DESKTOP COMPUTERS
AND PERSONAL SOFTWARE

The desktop computer had its earliest roots in the Xerox computer research lab in Palo Alto (known also as Xerox PARC). In the early 1970s, Alan Kay developed the metaphor of overlapping windows to hold data. The computer monitor suddenly developed depth and it became possible to visualize protein structures as a result of data in a database (Johnson, 1997). However, even these imaginative early systems were a far cry from today's modern notion of a computer desktop. More than another decade was required to create the graphical user interfaces that provide trash bins, file folders, icons, and menus, and full control of these objects with cursors controlled by hand operated pointing devices amusingly termed a *mouse*. By the early 1980s, Xerox had created the first modern desktop with the object-oriented language Smalltalk.

To some people, desktop computers revolutionized the way they worked. Here was a machine that could hold all of your important personal information and data, in a manner that was consistent with the way you worked. The data were now accessible at anytime by simply typing on a keyboard or pointing to an icon of a text or graphic document or a word or object within the document with a computer mouse. If that computer were connected to an Internet, you could now send and receive e-mail and files directly from your own personal computer. The software industry responded with an onslaught of software applications, some good, and some not so good. Databases were some of the better pieces of software that came out of this intense software development era. Scientists could now begin to organize their own pieces of data into some local system that was independent of the larger network and of the larger computers on the campus. Whole cottage industries began to form around the notion of organizing and protecting your personal data.

E-mail and FTP services were now available on the desktop computer by using software applications that were much more graphical and interactive. Graphical does not always mean easier, but in this case, the desktop computer used for e-mail and FTP made the experience easier. The files could be organized more easily into folders or file directories. Because the user controlled his own computer, and thus the local file system, the file system in essence became a sort of database for the user. It was quite commonplace to find the user organizing his files hierarchically in the computer according to some personal schema that he has in mind. The file system reflected his vision of his workflow. This seemed like a minor change in social habits, but in fact was an astounding leap forward in personal productivity.

The concept of databases was beginning to flow more easily into the speech of neuroscientists. They saw that the data gathered using technologically advanced laboratory systems had some sort of hierarchical arrangement. They saw that they could use, to a certain degree, their own personal computer's local file system to organize that data hierarchically. Commercial-quality database management systems became available for use on the personal computer. Databases were thus familiar to most neuroscientists without having had any specific training in their construction, operation, or utility. Neuroscientists are quite willing to employ expensive instrumentation to acquire and display their data (Hasman, 1987), and to explore the use of personal computers in the organization, access, and retrieval of their valuable data. The entire mindset beginning to develop at that time was extraordinary. Because more data than ever before could now be stored and accessed with great ease, neuroscientists began to focus more on the intrinsics of the data themselves. Scientists began to ask questions that really were the foundations of the scientific method, that is, creating the proper environments that would lead to successful data collection, reasoning, interpretation, replication, and acceptance of their findings.

PERSONAL COMPUTING SYSTEMS PROVIDE ASSISTANCE TO NEUROANATOMIC RESEARCH

There were two primary issues in our minds at the time we began to develop tools for this community: What are the primary data of morphologic research, and how are these observations replicated? Traditional morphologic data, such as that derived from the microscope, were virtually only assessed subjectively. Findings were compared, compiled, and transformed into an eventual publishable form more-or-less wholly from a story developing in the mind of the microscopist and exemplified by occasional photomicrographs or schematic drawings. Thus, the data in a published paper tended to be derived, selected, reduced, and interpreted. The gap between the raw observed data and the published, publicly viewable data could be enormous. Yet, for decades, this has been the manner in which the data are brought from the laboratory benchtop to the desktop of the scientific readership.

Part of the reason is that the final picture in published form is easier to comprehend than the mountains of raw data from which it is conceived. But with the technological systems beginning to be put into place in the modern neuroscience laboratory, those data could be just as easily viewed and interpreted by all scientists, and not just by the originator. Still, the mental transformation from morphological observation to data to conclusions is mysterious to nonmorphologists who nevertheless require morphological constraints to interpret their own chemical or physiological observations. This transformation may also be misleading to the observer–interpreter because the conclusions may not in fact be based on a broad sampling of the available data, but rather on the degree to which the observed patterns match a preconceived or rapidly formulated impression.

The scientific method requires that observations be verifiable by replication in order to confirm or reinterpret the conclusions of a study. Because the data are now beginning to be acquired in some electronic form, and because the use of the software applications that created the data are now much more prevalent and easy to use, such raw data can be reinterpreted by all scientists. The gap between raw data and published works begins to close somewhat. Social networks of scientists get tighter within local domains, but broader with respect to what they can now access and understand outside of their own domains of understanding.

THE NEED FOR BETTER NEUROSCIENTIFIC DATABASES

A common experience, especially after returning from an annual meeting of the Society for Neurosciences for example, is a perception of data-overload in which the facts reported and recalled are unlinked, unorganized, and almost unretrievable. The coordination of the new data and their possible informational value remain separated from the conceptual organization of that information or the implicit knowledge that the scholar brought to the meeting. Moreover, the knowledge in a given scholar's head is clearly only a portion of the available data in the literature with which that scientist is able to be familiar. That part of the literature base may be as broad or as narrow as the interests, time, and capacity of the scientist dictates. Whether the facts are seen and unappreciated or merely remain for the moment unseen, a formidable barrier exists between the existing collection of reported data, and the information and knowledge they may permit a scholar to formulate.

Without offering any factual documentation of the data explosion in neurosciences beyond the well-appreciated growth in the numbers of journals and the numbers of meetings, the general needs for a brain database will be obvious. A database would make possible the improved utilization of what exists in the literature, the comparison among collections of data, and the evaluation of conflicting conclusions and hypotheses. A database could be expected to reduce redundancy or it could potentially generate experiments designed to fill gaps revealed when the existing landscape of data is more thoroughly appreciated. Moreover, a database that would permit the creation of linkages between data collections would be expected to be heuristic in many directions, from evolving new experimental questions to evaluating new concepts of pathophysiology or new routes of treatment.

However, although the advantageous outcomes for both scholarship and for health applications are obvious, the manpower, hardware, and economic costs are equally daunting. For example, assembling the proper architecture of a brain database intended for broad scientific and clinical utility and entering the existing data into it, and maintaining currently accurate datasets, is what the press might call a monumental undertaking. Such an undertaking has so far defied implementation. Although computerized information management has taken hold for literature surveys, and for specific molecular comparisons, the very large number of different brain entities, relationships, and user interests combined with the extraordinarily large base of data and concepts, and conflicting, overlapping, and unrelated systems of nomenclature remain overwhelming intellectual obstacles. The costs of such a system will be significant although no exact costs can actually be estimated until the dimensions of such a project become defined. The means of distributing, updating and correcting the entries are also far from obvious. Regardless of the entities to be included and the attributes to be recorded, any database management team will also have to accommodate the wide base of user-selected computers already employed in academic environments.

A predictable outcome of all of the technological development, the application of this technology in the common neuroscience laboratory, the enabling of electronic collaboration, and the shortening of the gap between raw data and published data is the development of collaborative software projects whose goal is to enhance those community-based efforts. Our own efforts in this arena began in the late 1980s with a desire to create community databases. We wanted to couple this to morphological representations (brain atlases) of animal models so that there could be a common reference point for those raw data from which to compare other data from other collaboratories, and to draw similar or dissimilar conclusions that were based on heretofore agreed on conventions and formalities.

We would present this brain atlas or database as a research tool familiar to neuroscientists that we may regard as a graphical database in which entities are places listed in an index that refers the user to a given plate or series of drawings in one, two, or all three of the standard planes of section. This database is highly useful if you already know the name of the brain structure whose location you want to see, know enough about brain organization to relate that structure to other structures already known to you, and know enough about atlas navigation to look up these structures. However, an atlas is not very helpful if the name of the structure in the paper that evoked your search is not a naming term used by the authors of your atlas. Moreover, if you read the fine print introducing your atlas and learn that it is based on one 180 gram female Sprague-Dawley rat, how do you relate it to your research on 50 gram Wistar males? What if the place where your electrode tip is located is in between the two plates of the atlas showing this general area, and the plane of section of your specimen brain does not match the standard coordinate system?

AN EARLY MULTIDISCIPLINARY BRAIN DATABASE SYSTEM, THE BRAIN BROWSER™

Based on this reasoning, we developed a graphical user interface to The Rat Brain Atlas (Paxinos & Watson, 1987) using an Apple Macintosh computer and Apple HyperCard as the programming environment. Brain Browser (Bloom, Young, & Kim, 1989; Bloom & Young, 1993) contained a very easy to use interface to four modules that provided a tutorial to brain circuitry (Learner), a graphical representation of the rat brain atlas (NeuroNavigator), a set of plates that allowed one's own data to be superimposed on those atlas plates (DataMaker), and a database that supported the creation and searching of all neurocircuitry data (Linker). NeuroNavigator and Linker were the most used modules.

NeuroNavigator was a dynamic, living representation of the rat brain atlas. The individual plates from each of the three orthogonal planes (coronal, sagittal, and horizontal) were displayed very quickly on the computer. When the mouse cursor moved over certain areas in the brain section diagram, the locations and names of the underlying structures were automatically displayed. Their locations on plates in any of the orthogonal planes could be revealed instantly (see Fig. 6.1). Clicking on one of the 400+ locations automatically opened the correct structure card in Linker, displaying all the kinds of neurons in that location, their transmitters, receptors, afferents, and efferents, as well as the behavioral functions with which that location had been associated.

Selection of one of the 900+ afferent or efferent circuits would then take the user to a deeper level of information, displaying the details of the circuitry that linked to the original location, as well as the literature sources for the attributes described. In principle, a user who made a potential new discovery in the identification of transmitter, receptor or circuitry could immediately spot whether such a finding existed in the database. A user in search of something important to search for could scan the database for gaps in small or large details, of which there were many.

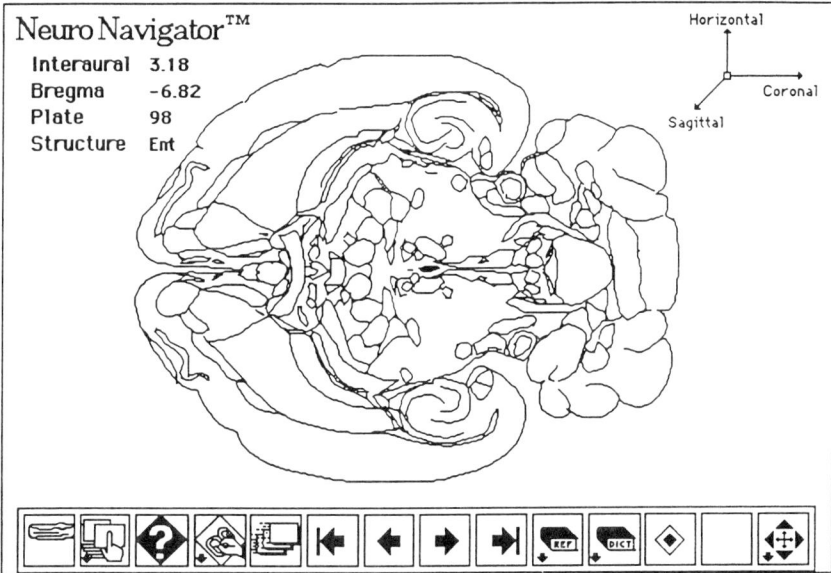

FIG. 6.1. This is a basic screen from Brain Browser showing a horizontal section from a rat brain. Moving the mouse over different sections of the plate displayed the know structure. Clicking the mouse button displayed the structure and circuitry information.

Although Brain Browser was certainly an interesting exercise in pushing the envelope in terms of information presentation in the late 1980s, it failed to gain significant interest beyond a few thousand users. The reasons were not obvious at the time, but are now, in light of other technologies that have also failed to gain favor. The main reason probably is lack of connectivity to external databases, and the inability to link the data in Brain Browser to live data continually being produced in the scientific community. Although there are importing and exporting tools in Brain Browser to support a community effort, they were too cumbersome for scientists to use on a periodic basis. Therefore, the predominant consumer of Brain Browser tended to use it more for personal uses, perhaps in laboratories or their own private Intranets, without the desire to couple it to a broader network of users, and not sharing those data with others.

Another reason for minimal community adaptation, perhaps, was that Brain Browser, while intuitively easy to use, and relatively quick and powerful in data searching and retrieval, fell by the wayside in deference to other, more exciting technologies, some of which have proven their merit (the Web), and others that were transient novelties (Silicon's Graphics' VRML, Apple's HotSauce, Kaleida, Taligent). Finally, the fact that the entire Brain Browser

package was wholly devoted to rat in an era when molecular neuroscience discoveries were also gaining significant momentum on murine and primate
brains may have been a part of the reason why the numerous purchasers of the
database system and its data failed to form a functional community.

THE INTERNET AND ELECTRONIC DATABASES

Not withstanding the efforts made by ourselves and others dedicated to developing standalone software, other developments in computer networking and
software quickly started another transition that neuroscientists needed to focus on. These efforts were enhanced by the creation of government programs
that were designed around large data gathering efforts, such as the Human
Genome Project (Cuticchia et al., 1993; Pearson & Söll, 1991) and the Human Brain Project (Huerta, Koslow, & Leshner, 1993). With the growth of the
neuroscience data, there is a need to create a comprehensive database of
neuronal circuitry for each of the major vertebrate central nervous systems as
tools to understand the known molecular, cellular, and macroscopic features
of the brains and their interspecies relationships. This database would be an
essential tool to understand the known molecular, cellular, and macroscopic
features of the brains and their interspecies relationships. Such a data management system is necessary to illuminate essential missing elements of information. As a consequence, our subsequent efforts, as well as those of many
others, have been dedicated to the development of a technology to combine
informatics (the science of data collection, organization, and interpretation)
with neuroscience with the goal of improved management and distribution of
neuroscience information.

Scientific interest in the neurosciences has grown enormously during the
late 1990s. That growth is evidenced by the membership in national societies
of neurosciences throughout the world, by the proliferation of scientific journals and magazines focused on the neurosciences, and by the programmatic
interests of a wide governmental and nongovernmental agencies. The sheer
volume of accumulated published original reviewed articles in the
neurosciences since the mid-1990s probably rivals that over the entire previous history of neuroscience research. At present, one can expect that the existing molecular discovery momentum will reveal in rich detail far more reliable
information on the detailed connections and mechanisms of interaction of
neuronal circuitry at the cellular and molecular levels of understanding.

One might note, for example, among recent discoveries, a wholly unexpected homolog of the now-classical hypothalamic neuropeptide,
somatostatin, discovered by searching for genes selectively expressed within
the hippocampus and cortex, and therefore termed cortistatin (de Lecea et al.,

1997). Physiological analysis of synthetic cortistatin revealed several functional differences from somatostatin (de Lecea et al., 1996). In a similar, region-selective search for new hypothalamic gene products (Gautvik et al., 1996) another neuropeptide was identified with a unique hypothalamic localization suggesting a role in visceral function (de Lecea et al., 1998), which was soon attributed to appetitive regulation and given the name orexin (Sakurai et al., 1998). A third example of this nature is the discovery of yet another unexpected neuropeptide, named CART by virtue of its enhanced expressed following treatment with c(une or amphetamine (Couceyro, Koylu, & Kuhar, 1997; Koylu et al., 1998; Koylu et al., 1997).

Thus, there can be little doubt that high quality data have expanded explosively in the neurosciences. However, there are several implicit barriers to the optimal utilization of this information. In particular, how can these myriad observations be converged into testable hypotheses of normal brain function or the molecular basis for any disease's neuropathogenesis? Because the transgenic mouse technology is providing tantalizing models for both Alzheimer's disease (Games et al., 1995; Hsiao et al., 1996; Masliah et al., 1996; Sturchler-Pierrat et al., 1997) and Amyotrophic Lateral Sclerosis (Morrison, Gordon, Ripps, & Morrison, 1996; Morrison, Janssen, Gordon, & Morrison, 1998; Ripps, Huntley, Horn, Morrison, & Gordon, 1995), this may be one successful approach to that convergence.

Aside from these pathological considerations, there is a striking need for serious scholarly attempts to model human cognitive operations through incorporation of rigorous data from chemical neuroanatomy and neurophysiology into modeling algorithms. However, when one seeks to do so, there is an immediate awareness that we lack reliable quantitative information on most aspects of human and experimental neuroanatomy. As noted by Cherniak (Cherniak, 1990), estimates published by highly regarded neuroscientists for such elemental factual considerations as the actual area or volume of the human cortex, the density of the neurons within this sheet, and the average number of synapses within the cortical neuropil differ by orders of magnitude. When one considers further the differences in brain shape between individuals, the difficulties in applying rigorously cytoarchitectonic and cortical connectivity criteria to define specific cortical regions, and the inability now to apply to human brain the connectivity tracing tools of experimental neuroanatomy (Crick & Jones, 1993), details of the structure and function of the human brain may appear unapproachable.

Quite apart from these pathological and quantitative correlates, there appear to be finite limits on the ability of any individual scientist to absorb, digest, and interpret the existing studies and to monitor, evaluate and incorporate new data into one's appreciation for a given brain region, system, or question. The characteristic motif of neuroscience, namely the interdisciplinary merging of data acquired by anatomists, chemists, and physiologists working at their preferred levels of resolution from the molecular to the organismic constitutes its own major barrier to substantive intellectual consolidation of the data.

TECHNOLOGY TOOLS FOR NEUROSCIENCE
DATA ACQUISITION

Paralleling the data explosion in the neurosciences is frustration in gathering reliable data. Although it is generally possible to retrieve relevant reliable information on brain molecules, one may be quickly stymied for information to understand the cell systems that express these genes and then to relate those genes and cells to the pertinent behaviors governed by these cells and cell systems. One hungers for a means to perform such vertical integrations of information (from the molecular to the behavioral) in a manner that would meet rigorous scientific standards and yet permit individual scholars the intellectual opportunity to conduct investigations of the accumulated data for their own specific relationships and for hypothesis generation. In our view, several sorts of information management tools are most needed and therefore motivate our efforts in this activity.

Another goal in the development of community software was an integrated software system for the quantitative acquisition, display, and analysis of cellular and subcellular morphological information from the microscope. The initial tool set of software ensemble, NeuroZoom, have already produced abundant quantitative information on a variety of neuronal markers in both experimental (Gazzaley, Siegel, Kordower, Mufson, & Morrison, 1996; Gazzaley, Weiland, McEwen, & Morrison, 1996; Gazzaley, Benson, Huntley, & Morrison, 1997; Hof & Morrison, 1995; Hof et al., 1995; Huntley et al., 1994; Nimchinsky, Morrison, & Schmauss, 1997; Nimchinsky, Huf, Young, & Morrison, 1996) and clinical (Hof, Bouras, Perl, & Morrison, 1994; Hof, Perl, Loerzel, Steele, & Morrison, 1994; Hof et al., 1995; Hof & Morrison, 1996; Hof, Bont, Bouras, & Morrison 1997) studies (see Figs. 6.2 & 6.3).

The advantage of using NeuroZoom is that all values in the database are obtained using stereological methods. These methods are mathematically derived and exceedingly robust (see Fig. 6.3). Another advantage is that these analyses are not complicated to perform. Thus, meaningful and definitive data are quickly obtained with these techniques. To realize its potential, such a data acquisition and analysis system should provide its data in a manner that can be integrated with a textual database management system. Only when these databases become an integral part of the literature awareness library of individual or working groups of scientists will improved scientific under-

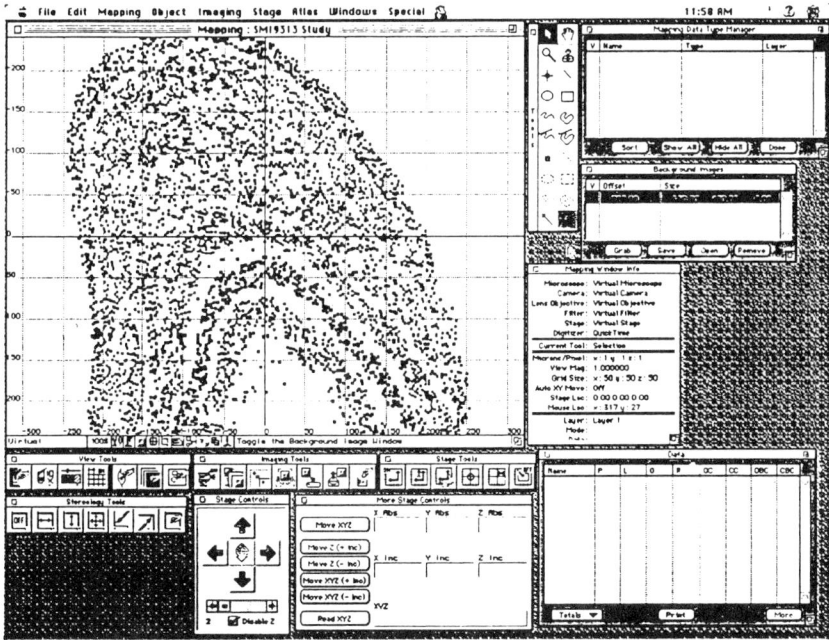

FIG. 6.2. This is the basic screen from NeuroZoom showing the cellular distribution of SMI containing cells mapped out using NeuroZoom tools. Color coding of the cells were used to highlight the different layers.

standing begin. Comparable tools are also required for the data obtained by neurochemical and neurophysiological research strategies, similarly tied to the cells and regions in which those facts are acquired.

One eventual goal for such tools is to provide the neuroscience scholar, regardless of prior experience, access to a computer or microscope system of their selection and the capability to move from the synaptic level, through cellular, multicellular (like layers of specific cortical areas or nuclei of defined subcortical locations), and regional microscopic levels up to the macroscopic framework of our atlases and databases within a quantitatively accurate, and platform (i.e., computer type) independent graphic display environment. Because experimental verification of detailed structural and functional information on human brains is unlikely to be obtainable, we look to the nonhuman primate brain as a likely experimental route through which human brain scholars could access the much richer database of neuronal circuitry, chemistry and cellular function in other species.

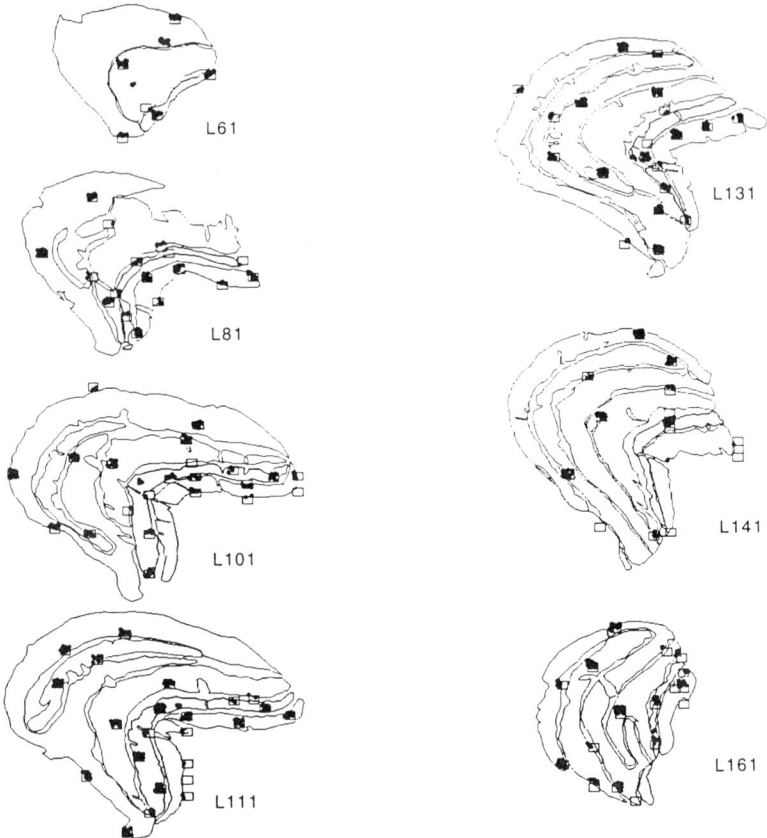

FIG. 6.3. These maps were produced using the stereological tools in NeuroZoom. The small colored boxes are sampled areas in Macaque monkey Lateral Geniculate Nucleus sections. The total number of cell bodies were estimated with this fraction.

MODELING THE BRAIN STRUCTURES
WITH DATABASES IN THE FUTURE

We are actively developing software to create and distribute an interactive Brain Object Database of the nervous system oriented within species on the templates representing the pages (electronically speaking) of a classical brain structural atlas. Comparisons of datasets across species are made with reference to the definable homologies between brain regional structures. Our working model, is composed of many of the standard classes of objects that are encountered in neurosciences, namely, neuroanatomic structures at various levels of resolution (from the top down: areas, regions, groups, nuclei, cells, cellular organelles, and macromolecules), neurochemical objects (from gene and mRNA sequences upward—in sizes—to proteins, organelles, and the regulatory molecular machinery for intracellular metabolic maintenance and intercellular transductive signaling) neurofunctional objects (cells, synapses, receptors, transductive mechanisms including ion channels, and their interactions on membrane properties) providing for cell–cell interactions in the sense of defined circuits.

Realistic classes of generic neurons are initially encoded with the actual known details of their generalized features, and enhanced by their exceptional properties, which may be defined when determined. Such biologically based neurons may then be collected into defined assemblies of neurons that represent any of the several defined functional systems. This collection can be applied to both normal and pathological states and carried from the molecular specifications up to the behavioral levels. We also envision such a data representational system to encode other neurodata objects (classical data renditions EEG, and Event-Related Potentials) as well as imaging modalities (MRI, PET, CAT, and MEG). This Brain Object Database will be constantly extendible in the classes of objects (molecules, organelles, neurons, neuronal subtypes, etc) and derived classes (circuits, circuit operations) based on the latest research information. Because the classes of objects and their relationships will be linked as life-like metaphors to their biological structures, the system can be suitable not only for encoding and comparing data across levels of analysis and species, but should also be suitable for work at the theoretical level of cellular or systems simulations.

In this manner, we are working to establish a truly comprehensive database that can link graphic image sets as well as textually-defined qualitative characteristics, based on progressively accumulated and refined (and eventually quantitatively established). The data would range from the level of whole brains down to the level of DNA and protein sequence, along with archival reference lists to papers containing those and other data and would lend itself to other online commentary forums. Eventually one can envision an ongoing global neuroscience forum for informal and cooperative data analysis and concept formulation among those collecting the data and those hungry for data to interpret.

COMPREHENSIVE CIRCUITRY DATABASES

Implementation of the database is also impacted by the circuitry data. The standard database model contains a framework in which specific data elements, as in spreadsheet cells, represent real objects (cells, nuclei, groups, area, etc.). Linkages are created between these objects as circuits, in which

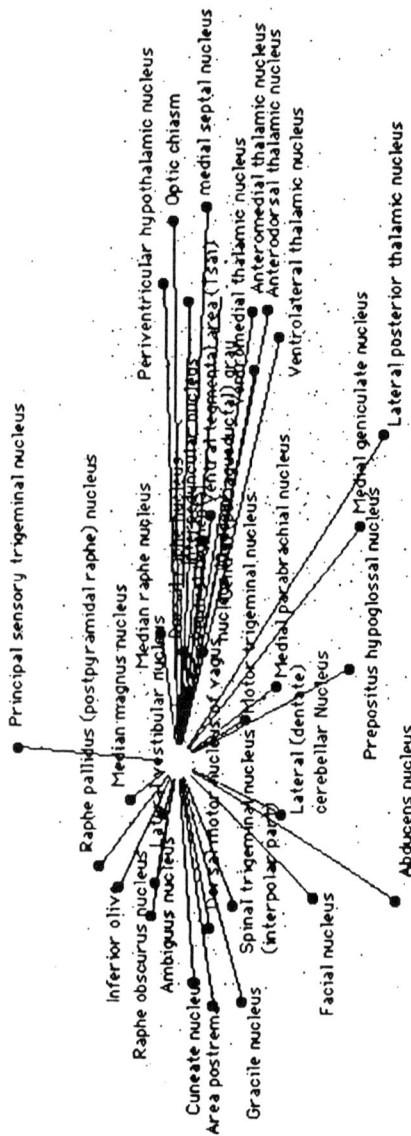

FIG. 6.4. This is a map representation in NeuroZoom of over 600 "Places" from the neurocircuitry database. One circuit was selected with locus coeruleus (yellow) projecting to its known targets (green). All other red dots are other places in the database.

each place can be any of the structural parts of the lineage as outlined above. Each place must then contain an additional attribute (database field) to act as a primary key to another place (see Fig. 6.4). However, several decades of research on neuronal circuitry makes it clear that the inter cellular structural and functional relationships already understood are far more complex than any existing database.

To search such a complex database for all known circuits falls into the classical highway algorithms in applications like telephone call routing. Brute force computation is required in this relational model to search all places, and to integrate this search until all end-nodes have been reached or some desired location is detected. Referential integrity of the database breaks down when data are redundant. Standard queries of circuits using relational technology are highly inefficient, because one rapidly reaches a point of diminishing returns. As the database content increases in depth with more and more samples, and in width with more attributes, the queries become much more time-consuming. Combine this with real-world access to the ideal database by multiple scientists, and any desired database access will likely experience poor performance.

We envision object database techniques as a ray of hope, potentially. The database in the simplest sense might be made up of a core engine that understands how to store and retrieve data from computer storage devices. The data that are stored or retrieved are almost always language independent. Basic raw data types are exchanged—strings, numbers, dates, currency, and long collections of binary data (Binary Large Object–BLOB). The basic data types are morphed into and out of the object language instances. So, a pyramidal cell or the visual area might have an efferent connection from the thalamus, or conversely, the thalamus might have an afferent connection to the visual area. This circuit could be represented in the database as three numbers. The first number would be a specific instance of the thalamus. The second number would indicate the afferent connection to the visual area. The third number would be a specific instance of the visual area itself. The numbers are obviously language independent, but when put back into the context of the place objects, they have anatomical meaning. Indeed, this is the same as for relational technology, except for one important difference—in relational technology, the software application is completely decoupled from the database. These data (the three numbers) must be retrieved from tables and rows using a query language, then programmatically inserted into a skeletal object (e.g., thalamus and visual area) to create the connection. Imagine doing this while traversing every pathway between the known source and the desired target. The computational load on the database engine increases tremendously. Conversely, when it is time to store the object into the database, the three numbers must be removed from the object, a query created for the relational database, and the numbers inserted into the proper tables and rows. Because of this decoupled nature, the responsibility of the software developer increases as well, as validation of the object in memory and the object in the database are manually maintained. The chance for error due to synchronization problems becomes significant.

An object database has the mechanisms in place to build the objects automatically whenever the software application tries to reference or use the object. There is no need to build the object by making a query, creating a skeletal object, and inserting the real values. The object database does this automatically. Therefore, the software programmer needs only to concern himself with the needs of the biologist, creating the special functions that a scientist would want, and to spend much less time dealing with database mechanics.

One promising object database management system is ObjectStore™ from Object Design, Inc. This package allows one to design the brain hierarchies completely using class definitions, represent the content with instances of each class, maintain cellular and circuitry specializations and variations with internal pointers in application memory, and have them stored persistently and transparently. To be optimally useful to society or a scientific community the database content may be distributed over a network in a transparent fashion. The database engines communicate with one another to determine where the data are located, and automatically forward references of the database objects to each other. Performance is very high. Storage capacities are in the pentabyte range. The circuit example outlined above can be at least 10 to 100 times faster than relational technology. Furthermore, because object technology is used throughout the database design, there are no restrictions on the data types that can be stored. Any data object that can be represented by the object language can be stored in the database. The class structures will be written in Java, and initial access to the database will be web enabled.

ENGAGING THE SCIENTIFIC COMMUNITY

Ultimately the users of this or some subsequent iteration of a whole brain database may decide to create an online intellectual community. Such a user group would share their common interest in linking human brain data pertinent to neurological and psychiatric diseases with the collected wisdom deducible from experimental brain research. To build such a group of users, and more particularly to induce them that the overall database effort is sufficiently attractive to invest their own time in getting their data into a form that can be entered into the database will require a community-debated and harmoniously formulated database masterplan, and with community-accepted standard descriptors as well as standards of rigor for data inclusion. Our experience with prior efforts to develop even primitive databases of this type for the rat (Bloom, Young, & Kim, 1989; Bloom & Young, 1993) is that widespread user acceptance is essential to the effective participation of the community to get data analyzed in ways suitable for inclusion in a database, and that the only way to achieve effective and active user participation is through progressive iteration and modification with potential users.

Thus, a driving justification for establishing an Brain Object-Database of realistic and modifiable objects representing real molecules in real linkages with other molecules, organelles, cells, circuits, and functions is that it will be realistic enough to attract data-producers and data-analysts. It should take on the significance of a deep knowledge system in which the pieces are not just mechanically linked, but rather contain realistic intellectual connections based on defined properties. Furthermore, the Brain Object Database can lead to a shared conceptual view of the brain, and of specific brains as a database suprastructure onto which new data, new linkages, and new concepts can be superimposed or incorporated.

The necessity for user acceptance, motivation, and participation also means to us that one cannot coerce users to any single form of computer platform. Thus, users should be free to use the device with which they are most comfortable, and in which they may already have substantial capital and intellectual investment. For that reason, we intend to use software that is portable across heterogeneous computer platforms such as the current favorite, Java™. This developmental environment would make the entire database and its class structures executable on virtually any computer presently used by neuroscientists.

The database environment we envision should also provide means to integrate the efforts of many individual neuroscientists, regardless of where they work. There is no question that research institutions are already well connected via the Internet, and that having tasted this new communication capacity has generated a boundless demand for higher speeds on new data superhighways. We envision the databases as being distributed among the neuroscientists such that database actions (such as searching for a specific combination of facts or diseases) will automatically be empowered to reach out into the world-wide network to retrieve the desired data with no more delay than if those data were already present within the network of the local research laboratory.

ELECTRONIC COLLABORATION
AND SCIENTIFIC PUBLISHERS

With all neuroscientists in the 1990s firmly rooted in the use of computers to assist them in their daily chores, and with software tools that help acquire, organize, and analyze data, there becomes increasingly obvious one of the few remaining links in the chain of data flow from the laboratory to the end-user. How do we get the data to the consumers more quickly? Certainly, electronic publication was not new in the 1990s. However, getting it organized in a way that was facile to the users, namely the scientists, and providing clever, but powerful tools proved much more daunting than what was originally thought. In the field of physics, Dr. Ginsparg in 1991 created a culture among his peers by publishing scientific works without peer review (Ginsparg, 1994, 1996). Scientists would post their findings on an Internet site so that others in the field could critique it over time. It was felt that the bad papers would be weeded out as part of this process, and the better ones would survive, and be quoted. This pretty much collapsed the traditional peer review process of original scientific work into a single publishing phase.

The process that worked well for physics would not work well for neurosciences. Partly because many disciplines in neurosciences require abstract, nonmathematical, and thus less formal interpretation of a data. Veteran peer reviewers in the field are needed to preview the work before general consumption. Furthermore, the sheer volume of neuroscience work made it very difficult to separate the noise from the signal. If all the neuroscience works were published without peer review in some electronic medium, the ability of

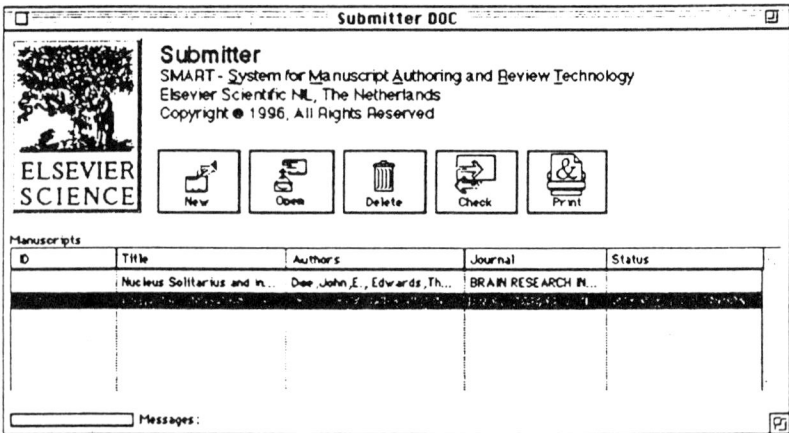

FIG. 6.5. SMARTWorks is an integrated set of programs designed to work together to support the submission of peer-reviewed Brain Research manuscripts through the review cycle. SMART Works uses the Internet as the connecting network among all users. Authors use certified commercial software applications to author their manuscripts. Information concerning the authors, paper format, journals, keywords, and manuscript files are assembled together into a package by SMART Works and transmitted through the Internet to a server. The review phase is initiated and selected reviewers electronically read and write their reviews. Advantages are greatly reduced time-to-review, time-to-publish, and time-to-read periods.

the neuroscience community to separate out the good from the bad would be difficult, if not impossible.

However, technology does provide empowerment in many aspects of the sciences. In one manner, networks and computers can be used to accelerate the process of peer review manuscripts. Since 1996, we have worked with Elsevier Scientific Publishers to develop an Internet-based submission and peer review system called SMART (System for Manuscript Authoring and Review Technology; see Fig. 6.5). It was originally written specifically for the Apple Macintosh computer, and eventually ported to a full web-based system. Launched in December 1997 for Brain Research Interactive, a new section of the brain research family of journals, it has since attracted more than 100 manuscript submissions in the first 9 months of use. All submissions are enabled electronically using any standard web browser from any computer, and initiates and facilitates the peer review using web browsers. In addition, the editorial office may track all manuscripts with a standard web browser.

One of the goals to using an electronic system from submission to publication is the easy integration of computer datasets into the published manuscript. It should be as easy to view electrophysiological data as it would be to read text, see an image, or click on a web link to another data source. For example, NeuroZoom data that is stored in its own data files may be selected from a computer window, highlighted, and dragged to a manuscript being created and submitted with SMART. The NeuroZoom data are then introduced into the manuscript. When reviewers or readers get to that part that represents the data, they need only click on it to launch a Web-enabled portion of NeuroZoom to open up and display that data in its own window on the user's computer. This entire process does not require the author to type any data at all. The data are acquired electronically using desktop computer software, such as NeuroZoom, graphically selected and placed in a manuscript that is being created on the computer, reviewed and accepted or declined by editorial staff, and then made available for consumption by the general neuroscience community. The entire phase of doing the experiment and publishing the results has been collapsed from about 6 months to a year, to days or hours. However, because the collaboratories allow for better communication among scientists, and because tools like NeuroZoom provide rigid methods of collecting and analyzing data, the quality of the neuroscience data increases while time to produce that data decreases.

THE FUTURE AND ITS IMPLICATIONS
FOR NEUROSCIENCES

Perhaps in this fashion, one may begin to change the information gathering habits of the neuroscientific community and allow the science to rise to even more powerful means to capture the information residing within today's data and to ask more heuristic questions tomorrow. A user-friendly "deep knowledge" database is the ultimate goal. This would be a database of brain information that transcended levels of resolution (molecules to cells to systems to behaviors). It would also have to transcend grouped members of a species of brain. The Brain Object Database should also be operated in conjunction with an intelligent data filtering, indexing, and database entry system. In that way, interested users could in fact stay on top of current information that matches their user-defined profiles of interest and to which new interest elements can later be defined, dropped, or reassigned. Both parts of this neuroscientific communications solution are necessary to solve the current information problem. We have only spoken here about the database tools, the data gathering tools, and the data publishing tools. We have seen enormous changes come about in how neuroscientists work. We have seen social behavior change, such as with the increased use of electronic publishing. We have seen better science as a result of rigorous tools whose validity has been proven over time.

Neuroscientists of the future will likely look back on the 1990s as a time of primitive computing skills. The decade will be considered perhaps as the beginning passage across an informational threshold from a time when printed textbooks held all the important qualitative introductory concepts of chemistry, circuitry, transductive signaling, and the hypothetical biology underlying emotional and cognitive operations. The neuroscientist of the 21st century will wonder how those pioneers ever established that an experimental perturbation actually made significant differences without having normative tables of neuronal number, morphology, afferent and efferent circuitry densities, and gene expression patterns for every location in every common strain of mouse and rat brain. The clinical neuroscientists of the 21st century will be amazed that there was any inferential impact of those rodent data on human neuropsychopathology without the ability to reason accurately across the vast differences in human brain macrostructures to the underlying genetic and chemical differences in need of therapeutic adjustment. One wishes earnestly to survive to those times to see how that transition was made.

REFERENCES

Agnati, L. F., Fuxe, K., Goldstein, L. C. M., Toffano, G., Giardino, L., & Zoli, M. Computer-assisted morphometry and microdensitometry of transmitter-identified neurons with special reference to the mesostriatal dopamine pathway. II. Further studies on the effects of the GM1 ganglioside on the degenerative and regenerative features of mesostriatal dopamine neurons. *Acta Physiol. Scand. 122*, 37–44.

Bloom, F. E. (1995). Neuroscience-knowledge management: Slow change so far. *Trends Neurosci, 18*(2), 48–49.

Bloom, F. E., & Young, W. G. (1993). *Brain browser™ for Windows*. San Diego, CA: Academic Press.

Bloom, F. E., & Young, W. G. (1994). New solutions for neuroscience communications are still needed. *Prog. Brain Res. 100*, 275–281.

Bloom, F. E., Young, W. G., & Kim, Y. (1989). *Brain browser*. San Diego, CA: Academic Press.

Capowski, J. J. (1983). An automatic neuron reconstruction system. *J. Neurosci. Methods, 8*, 353–364.

Capowski, J. J. (1977). Computer-aided reconstruction of neuron trees from several serial sections. *Computers and Biomedical Research, 10*, 617.

Capowski, J. J., & Rethelyi, M. (1978).Computer analysis of the distribution of synaptic elements of Golgi-stained axon trees. *Brain Theory Newsletter, 3*, 179.

Capowski, J. J., & Sedivec, M. J. (1981). Accurate computer reconstruction and graphics display of complex neurons utilizing state of the art interactive techniques. *Computers in Biomedical Research, 14*, 518.

Cherniak, C. (1990). The bounded brain: toward quantitative neuroanatomy. *J. Cog. Neurosci., 2*, 58–68.

Couceyro, P. R., Koylu, E. O., & Kuhar, M. J. (1997). Further studies on the anatomical distribution of CART by in situ hybridization. *J. Chem. Neuroanat., 12*(4), 229–241.

Crick, F., & Jones, E. G. (1993). Backwardness of human neuroanatomy. *Nature, 361*, 109–110.

Cuticchia, A. J., Chipperfield, M. A., Porter, C. J., Kearns, W., & Pearson, P. L. (1993). Managing all those bytes: The human genome project. *Science, 262*, 47–48.

de Lecea, L., Criado, J. R., Prospero-Garcia, O., Gautvik, K. M., Schweitzer, P., Danielson, P. E., Dunlop, C. L., Siggins, G. R., Henriksen, S. J., & Sutcliffe, J. G. (1996). A cortical neuropeptide with neuronal depressant and sleep-modulating properties. *Nature, 381*(6579), 242–245.

de Lecea, L., del Rio, J. A., Criado, J. R., Alcantara,S., Morales, M., Danielson, P. E., Henriksen, S. J., Soriano, E., & Sutcliffe, J. G. (1997). Cortistatin is expressed in a distinct subset of cortical interneurons. *J. Neurosci, 17*(15), 5868–5880.

de Lecea, L., Kilduff, T. S., Peyron, C., Gao, X., Foye, P. E., Danielson, P. E., Fukuhara, C., Battenberg, E. L., Gautvik, V. T., Bartlett, F. S. (1998). The hypocretins: Hypothalamus-specific peptides with neuroexcitatory activity. *Proc. Natl. Acad. Sci. U.S.A., 95*(1):322–327.

DuVarney, D., & DuVarney, R. C. (1985). A computer-base video microscope for cell measurement. In R. Mize (Ed.), *The microcomputer in cell and neurobiology research*. Elsevier Science Publishing.

Eidelberg, E., & Davis, F. (1997). An improved electronic pantograph. *J. Histochem. Cytochem, 25*, 1016–1018.

Foote, S. L., Loughlin, S. E., Cohen, P. S., Bloom, F. E., & Livingston, R. B. (1980). Accurate three-dimensional reconstruction of neuronal distributions in brain: reconstruction of the rat nucleus locus coeruleus. *J. Neurosci. Meth., 3*, 159–173.

Forbes, D. J., & Petry, R. W. (1979). Computer-assisted mapping with the light microscope. *J. Neurosci. Meth., 1*, 77–94.

Gallistel, C. R., Piner, C. T., Allen, T. O., Adler, N. T., Yadin, E., & Negin, M. (1982). Computer assisted analysis of 2–DG autoradiographs. *Neurosci. Biobehav. Rev., 6,* 409–420.

Games, D., Adams, D., Alessandrini, R., Barbour, R., Berthelette, P., Blackwell, C., Carr, T., Clemens, J., Donaldson, T., Gillespie, F., et al. (1995). Alzheimer-type neuropathology in transgenic mice overexpressing V717F beta-amyloid precursor protein [see comments]. *Nature, 373*(6514), 523–527.

Gautvik, K. M., de Lecea, L., Gautvik, V. T., Danielson, P. E., Tranque, P., Dopazo, A., Bloom, F. E., & Sutcliffe, J. G. (1996). Overview of the most prevalent hypothalamus-specific mRNAs, as identified by directional tag PCR subtraction. *Proc. Natl. Acad. Sci. U.S.A., 93*(16): 8733–8738.

Gazzaley, A. H., Benson, D. L., Huntley, G. W., & Morrison, J. H. (1997). Differential subcellular regulation of NMDAR1 protein and mRNA in dendrites of dentate gyrus granule cells after perforant path transection. *J. Neurosci., 17*(6), 2006–2017.

Gazzaley, A. H., Siegel, S. J., Kordower, J. H., Mufson, E. J., & Morrison, J. H. (1996). Circuit-specific alterations of N-methyl-D-aspartate receptor subunit 1 in the dentate gyrus of aged monkeys. *Proc. Natl. Acad. Sci. U.S.A., 93*(7), 3121–3125.

Gazzaley, A. H., Weiland, N. G., McEwen, B. S., & Morrison, J. H. (1996). Differential regulation of NMDAR1 mRNA and protein by estradiol in the rat hippocampus. *J Neurosci. 16*(21), 6830–6838.

Ginsparg, P. (1994). *Computers in Physics, 8,* 390.

Ginsparg, P. (1996, February). In Electronic Publishing in Science, Joint ICSU Press/UNESCO Conference, Paris, France.

Glaser, E. M., Gissler, M., & Van der Loos, H. (1979,). An interactive camera lucida computer-assisted microscope. In Annual Meeting Soc. Neurosci. Atlanta, GA.

Goochee, C., Rasband, W., & Sokoloff, L. (1979). Computerized densitometry and color coding of 14C-deoxyglucose autoradiographs. *Ann. Neurol. 7,* 359–370.

Green, J. O. (1997). *The new age of communications.* New York, NY: Henry Holt and Company.

Harnad, S. (1990). Scholarly skywriting and the prepublication continuum of scientific inquiry. *Psychological Science, 1,* 342–343.

Hasman, A. (1987) Medical applications of computers: An overview. *Int J Biomed Comput, 20,* 239–51.

Hibbard, L. S., & Hawkins, R. A. (1984). Three-dimensional reconstruction of metabolic data from quantitative autoradiography of rat brain. *Am. J. Physiol. 47,* E412–E419, 1984.

Hillman, E. E. (1977). A tridimensional reconstruction computer system for neuroanatomy. *Computer Medicine., 5,* 1.

Hof, P. R., & Morrison, J. H. (1995). Neurofilament protein defines regional patterns of cortical organization in the macaque monkey visual system: a quantitative immunohistochemical analysis. *J Comp. Neurol., 352*(2), 161–186.

Hof, P. R., & Morrison, J. H. (1996). Hippocampal and neocortical involvement in normal brain aging and dementia: Morphological and neurochemical profile of the vulnerable circuits. *J. Am. Geriatr. Soc., 44*(7), 857–864.

Hof, P. R., Bouras, C., Perl, D. P., & Morrison, J. H. (1994). Quantitative neuropathologic analysis of Pick's disease cases: cortical distribution of Pick bodies and coexistence with Alzheimer's disease [see comments]. *Acta Neuropathol., 87*(2), 115–124.

Hof, P. R., Bouras, C., Perl, D. P., Sparks, D. L., Mehta, N., & Morrison, J. H. (1995). Age-related distribution of neuropathologic changes in the cerebral cortex of patients with Down's syndrome. Quantitative regional analysis and comparison with Alzheimer's disease. *Arch. Neurol., 52*(4), 379–391.

Hof, P. R., Nimchinsky, E. A., & Morrison, J. H. (1995). Neurochemical phenotype of corticocortical connections in the macaque monkey: Quantitative analysis of a subset of neurofilament protein-immunoreactive projection neurons in frontal, parietal, temporal, and cingulate cortices. *J. Comp Neurol., 362*(1), 109–133.

Hof, P. R., Perl, D. P., Loerzel, A. J., Steele, J. C., & Morrison, J. H. (1994). Amyotrophic lateral sclerosis and parkinsonism-dementia from Guam: Differences in neurofibrillary tangle distribution and density in the hippocampal formation and neocortex. *Brain Res., 650*(1), 107–116.

Hof, P. R., Vogt, B. A., Bouras, C., & Morrison, J. H. (1997). Atypical form of Alzheimer's disease with prominent posterior cortical atrophy: A review of lesion distribution and circuit disconnection in cortical visual pathways. *Vision Res., 37*(24), 3609–3625.

Hsiao, K., Chapman, P., Nilsen, S., Eckman, C., Harigaya, Y., Younkin, S., Yang, F., & Cole, G. (1996). Correlative memory deficits, A beta elevation, and amyloid plaques in transgenic mice [see comments]. *Science, 274*(5284), 99–102.

Huerta, M. F., Koslow, S. H., & Leshner, A. I. (1993). The human brain project: an international resource. *Trends in Neurosciences, 16*, 436–438.

Huntley, G. W., Vickers, J. C., Janssen, W., Brose, N., Heinemann, S. F., & Morrison, J. H. (1994). Distribution and synaptic localization of immunocytochemically identified NMDA receptor subunit proteins in sensory-motor and visual cortices of monkey and human. *J Neurosci., 14*(6), 3603–3619.

Johnson, S (1997). Interface culture: How new technology transforms the way we create and communicate. New York, NY: HarperCollins Publishers.

Koylu, E. O., Couceyro, P. R., Lambert, P. D., Ling, N. C., DeSouza, E. B., & Kuhar, M. J. (1997). Immunohistochemical localization of novel CART peptides in rat hypothalamus, pituitary and adrenal gland. *J. Neuroendocrinol., 9*(11), 823–833.

Koylu, E. O., Couceyro, P. R., Lambert, P. D., & Kuhar, M. J. (1998). Cocaine- and amphetamine-regulated transcript peptide immunohistochemical localization in the rat brain. *J. Comp. Neurol., 391*(1), 115–132.

Lindsay, R. D. (1977). The video computer microscope and A. R. G. O. S. In R. D. Lindsay (Ed.), Computer analysis of neuronal structures (computers in biology and medicine). New York, NY: Plenum Press.

Macagno, E. R., Leventhal, C., & Sobel, I. (1979). Three dimensional computer reconstruction of neurons and neuronal assemblies. *Annual Rev. Biophys. Bioeng., 8*, 323.

Mara, M. A., Hillier, L., & Waterston, R. H. (1998). Expressed sequence tags- Establishing bridges between gnomes. *Trends in Genetics, 14*(1), 4–7.

Masliah, E., Sisk, A., Mallory, M., Mucke, L., Schenk, D., & Games, D. (1996). Comparison of neurodegenerative pathology in transgenic mice overexpressing V717F beta-amyloid precursor protein and Alzheimer's disease. *J. Neurosci., 16*(18), 5795–5811.

McEachron, D. L., Gallistel, C. R., Eilbert, J. L., & Tretiak, O. J. (1988). The analytic and functional accuracy of a video densitometry system. *J. Neurosci. Meth., 25*, 63–74.

Mize, R. R., Holdefer, R. N., & Nabors, L. B. (1988). Quantitative immunocytochemistry using an image analyzer. I. Hardware evaluation, image processing, and data analysis. *J. Neurosci. Meth., 26*, 1–24.

Morrison, B. M., Gordon, J. W., Ripps, M. E., & Morrison, J. H. (1996). Quantitative immunocytochemical analysis of the spinal cord in G86R superoxide dismutase transgenic mice: neurochemical correlates of selective vulnerability. *J. Comp. Neurol., 373*(4), 619–631.

Morrison, B. M., Janssen, W.G., Gordon, J. W., & Morrison, J. H. (1998). Time course of neuropathology in the spinal cord of G86R superoxide dismutase transgenic mice. *J. Comp. Neurol., 391*(1), 64–77.

Nimchinsky, E. A., Hof, P. R., Janssen, W.G. M., Morrison, J. H., & Schmauss, C. (1997). Expression of dopamine D3 receptor dimers and tetramers in brain and in transfected cells. *J. Biol. Chem., 272*(46), 29229–29237.

Nimchinsky, E. A., Hof, P. R., Young, W.G., & Morrison, J. H. (1996). Neurochemical, morphologic, and laminar characterization of cortical projection neurons in the cingulate motor areas of the macaque monkey. *J Comp Neurol., 374*(1), 136–160.

Nowakowski, R. S. (1989). A Multi–User Imaging System for Research in Neurobiology. *Advanced Imaging., 4*(7), 44–48.

Palacios, J. M., Niehoff, D. L., & Kuhar, M. J. (1981). Receptor autoradiography with tritium-sensitive film: potential for computerized densitometry. *Neurosci. Lett, 25*, 101–105.

Part, M. R. (1985). A Completely Digital Neurophysiological Recording Laboratory. In R. Mize (Ed.), The microcomputer in cell and neurobiology research. Elsevier Science Publishing Co.

Paxinos, G., & Watson, C. (1987). The rat brain in stereotaxic coordinates. (2nd ed.) San Diego, CA: Academic Press.

Pearson, M. L., & Söll, D. (1991). The human genome project: A paradigm for information management in the life sciences. *FASEB J., 5*(1), 35–39.

Reuman, S. R., & Capowski, J. J. (1984). Automated neuron tracing using the Marr-Hildereth Zerocrossing technique. *Computers and Biomedical Research, 17*, 93–115.

Ripps, M. E., Huntley, G. W., Hof, P. R., Morrison, J. H., & Gordon, J. W. (1995). Transgenic mice expressing an altered murine superoxide dismutase gene provide an animal model of amyotrophic lateral sclerosis. *Proc Natl Acad Sci USA, 92*(3), 689–693.

Sakurai, T., Amemiya, A., Ishii , M., Matsuzaki, I., Chemelli, R. M., Tanaka, H., Williams, S. C., Richardson, J. A., Kozlowski, G. P., Wilson, S., et al. (1998). Orexins and orexin receptors: A family of hypothalamic neuropeptides and G protein-coupled receptors that regulate feeding behavior [see comments]. *Cell, 92*(4), 573–585.

Sturchler-Pierrat, C., Abramowski, D., Duke, M., Wiederhold, K. H., Mistl, C., Rothacher, S., Ledermann, B., Burki, K., Frey, P., Paganetti, P. A., et al. (1997). Two amyloid precursor protein transgenic mouse models with Alzheimer disease-like pathology. *Proc. Natl. Acad. Sci. U.S.A., 94*(24), 13287–13292.

Toga, A. W., & Arnicar-Sulze, T. L. (1987). Digital image reconstruction for the study of brain structure and function. *J. Neurosci. Meth., 20,* 7–21; 1987.

Toga, A. W., Santori, E. M., & Samaie, M. (1986). Regional distribution of flunitrazepam binding constants: Visualizing Kd and Bmax by digital image analysis. *J. Neurosci., 6,* 2747–2756.

Woolsey, T. A., & Dierker, M. L. (1998). Computer-assisted recording of neuroanatomical data. In R. T. Robertson (Ed.), Neuroanatomical research techniques, (pp. 48–85). New York, NY: Academic Press.

Wulf, W. (1993). *Committee on a National Collaboratory, Computer Science and Telecommunications Board, National Research Council, National Collaboratories: Applying Information Technology for Scientific Research.* Washington, DC: National Academy Press.

Young, W. G., Morrison, J. H., & Bloom, F. E. (1985). An electronic morphometry and mapping analysis microscopy system (EMMA) for the quantitative and comparative study of neurostructures. *Soc. Neurosci. Abstr., 11,* 679.

Author Index

Subject Index